"But of that day and hour no one knows, not even
the angels of heaven, but My Father only. . . .
Therefore you also be ready, for the Son of Man
is coming at an hour you do not expect."

Matthew 24:36, 44

MANY PEOPLE WANT TO UNDERSTAND HOW THE RAPTURE UNFOLDS, AND
this is the perfect handbook to share with those you love—
friends and family, as well as any others you know who are
still seeking the Truth—so they can prepare themselves before
the Rapture, or cope with, the challenges they'll face after the
Rapture. With trusted biblical insight, this book will provide the
hope and confidence you need and can share with your loved
ones. Throughout this book it is my honor to offer these prayers
for you and for you to join me in these prayers—seeking God's
peace, love, and forgiveness, and coming to know Jesus as your
Lord and Savior.

Dr. David Jeremiah

AFTER THE RAPTURE

AFTER THE RAPTURE

AN END TIMES GUIDE TO SURVIVAL

DR. DAVID JEREMIAH

W PUBLISHING GROUP

Library of Congress Cataloging-in-Publication Data

Names: Jeremiah, David, 1941- author.
Title: After the rapture : an end times guide to survival / David Jeremiah.
Description: Nashville, Tennessee : W Publishing, [2022] | Summary: "What if you or someone you loved missed out on the Rapture? What happens to those who are left behind? Trusted and beloved Bible teacher Dr. David Jeremiah shares the help and hope people will need as they face unfolding events during the End Times"-- Provided by publisher.
Identifiers: LCCN 2022011200 | ISBN 9780785292340 (trade paperback) | ISBN 9780785292357 (epub)
Subjects: LCSH: End of the world. | Rapture (Christian eschatology)
Classification: LCC BT877 .J47 2022 | DDC 236/.9--dc23/eng/20220321
LC record available at https://lccn.loc.gov/2022011200

Printed in the United States of America

22 23 24 25 26 LSC 10 9 8 7 6 5 4

CONTENTS

INTRODUCTION

LIGHT IN THE DARKNESS

ONE OF THE OLDEST WORKS OF ART IN THE US CAPITOL IS FOUND IN THE entrance to Statuary Hall, which was the original chambers for the House of Representatives. It's a huge timepiece called the *Car of History* clock. Situated above the clock is Clio, the muse of history. She holds a book in which she records events as they unfold. Created by Carlo Franzoni, the clockwork was installed in 1837 by Simon Willard.

Historian and Pulitzer Prize–winner David McCullough, while delivering a speech before a joint session of Congress in 1989, pointed to the clock and poignantly stated, "It is also a clock with two hands and an old-fashioned face. The kind that shows what time it is now . . . what time it used to be . . . what time it will become."[1]

The hands on God's prophetic clock tell us "what time it will become," and they are quickly moving toward midnight. The times are urgent, the days are short, and the battle is fierce. The darkness is closing in. But thank God there is a place you can find light.

The ancient prophecies of the Bible are God's floodlight on the future. But why turn to the Bible for light? What sets the Bible apart from all other religious books and writings? The answer is simple, yet profound. In the pages of the Bible there are approximately one thousand prophecies, more than half of which have already been literally, accurately fulfilled. The rest of the prophecies are in the process of being fulfilled before our eyes. Not one prophecy in the Bible has ever failed. The Bible has an astounding, unparalleled track record of forecasting what lies ahead in the darkness. Nothing else is even close. Only the Bible can accurately tell us "what time will become" in the days ahead. For this reason the Bible serves as our prophetic light to discern the future of the world and our own future.

The sequence of end-time events presented in this book is based on the premise that the Rapture—the sudden catching away of all believers in Jesus to heaven—is the initial event of the end times and that the Rapture has already happened. That with the occurrence of the Rapture, the prophetic trigger will have been pulled. That there's no stopping the series of end-time events that will ensue.

If that view is correct, and I'm convinced it is, you may be reading these words *after the Rapture*. But you may be reading this before these foretold events occur. Or you may be reading these words and reeling in the immediate aftermath of the mass vanishing. Or you may be reading these words several months or even years after the vanishing. Regardless of when you're reading, this book covers events that will happen to those who are part of the terminal generation when time is short, very short, and there is no way to avoid what's coming.

I know that sounds ominous, but it's true. At this point there is no reason to tiptoe around the truth. If you're reading these words after the disappearance of millions of people (the Rapture), you are part of the generation that will experience a series of cascading calamities unlike anything in the annals of human history. The world is on the precipice of a plunge into a time of unparalleled trouble. Jesus spoke of this terminal generation two millennia ago when He said, "Even so, when you see all these things, you know that it is near, right at the door. Truly I tell you, this generation will certainly not pass away until all these things have happened" (Matthew 24:33–34 NIV).

What's happening around you is undoubtedly traumatizing and deeply disturbing. You may feel like you're in the cast of an apocalyptic movie set in a dystopic future. I'm sure you have found yourself asking questions you've never asked before and never dreamed you would be asking. Even so, no matter how ominous things look, God is still in control and holds the future in His hands. God is the director and producer of the final drama. As Sinclair Ferguson reminds us, "That is why we can be quietly confident—not because we know exactly what God is doing in this unpredictable world, but because we know that what is unpredictable to us is already predicted by Him."[2]

Someone, maybe a relative or close friend who cares about you deeply, may have given you this book and asked you to read it in the event people all over the world vanish in a split second of time. Perhaps you picked it up because you are shocked, afraid, and confused about what's happening and what lies ahead. Or maybe your curiosity has been piqued and you are reading this book *before* the vanishing of millions of people all over the globe. No matter *why* you're reading this book or *when* you're reading it, you're probably wondering, *Is there hope?* I can answer with a definite and resounding, "Yes!"

I wrote this book for you with one simple purpose in mind: to give you hope in the darkness. You must, however, take care that your hope is accurately placed. You must put your hope in Jesus Christ. Please know that I have prayed earnestly for you that this book would find its way into your hands and that God will use this book to shine the light of Jesus Christ into your heart.

During the French Revolution, political prisoners were herded into dungeons. In one cell a prisoner had a Bible. His cell was crammed with men who wanted to hear the Word of God.

Once each day, for only a few moments, a shaft of light would come through a tiny window near the ceiling. The prisoners devised a plan whereby they would lift the owner of the Bible on their shoulders and into the sunlight. There, in that position, he would study the Scriptures. Then they would lower him down and say, "Tell us now, friend, what did you read while you were in the light?"[3]

You may feel like one of those prisoners right now, trapped and losing hope. But I pray you will allow me to share with you what I have read in God's Word while I was in the light. Please keep reading and ask God to open your heart to what He has to say to you.

Tom Perrotta's novel *The Leftovers*, also made into an HBO series, "starts with this premise: What if suddenly millions of people instantaneously vanished around the world in a scenario similar to but definitely different from the biblical event known as the Rapture? Those left behind are called the leftovers. Perrotta writes about how they cope with grief and loss and why some see this as an act of God and believe it's the start of the end times while others struggle to find ways to live with the inexplicable."[1]

What you are living through right now is definitely not fiction, but you, too, are probably struggling to find ways to grasp the inexplicable, wondering if what has happened has something to do with the end times. I can assure you it does. I'm so glad you are reading this book. There is nothing more important in this moment than for you to understand what has just happened and what it means for your future and the future of the world.

1

WHAT ON EARTH JUST HAPPENED?

ON SEPTEMBER 11, 2001, A RESTAURANT WORKER IN NEW YORK CITY went into the large walk-in refrigerator and closed the door behind him. When he emerged about fifteen minutes later, nobody was there. The restaurant was empty—no kitchen staff, no waiters, nobody was there. Confused, he wondered where they all could have gone. Then he noticed water leaking out of a crack in the ceiling and wall.

Suddenly, a man burst into the restaurant with a crazed look in his eyes. The restaurant worker, pointing to the cracked ceiling, told the man, "You can't come in here; it's not safe."

The man replied, "Just go look . . . Just go look . . . Go outside and look."

The restaurant worker went outside into the courtyard . . .

and nobody was there. In stunned silence, he had no idea what had happened. All he knew was that in the brief span of fifteen minutes, everything had changed. Sealed in a soundproof walk-in refrigerator at ground zero, he had missed the initial impact of 9/11. He emerged to discover a totally new world.[2]

Like that restaurant worker, you may not have personally witnessed the vanishing of millions of people from the face of the earth. You may have been asleep at night when the world changed forever. Perhaps you woke up and walked out into a shocking new world. Cable news, your cell phone, and social media were blowing up. You were trying to make sense of it all. Or you may have been alone somewhere and did not witness people disappear into thin air.

Or perhaps, like those who witnessed 9/11 firsthand, you may have been awake and going about your life when out of nowhere the world changed forever as people around you vanished in broad daylight. One second they were there; the next second they were gone—and people everywhere were dazed, frozen in place, their eyes fixed to the sky.

When or how you discovered what happened, you couldn't believe what you were seeing and hearing. Millions were mysteriously missing. People all over the planet disappeared in a split second. You quickly recognized that the world would never be the same. Everything changed in a flash. There has never been anything like this—not even close. To say the world is stunned and bewildered is a colossal understatement. Untold chaos has ensued. Confusion reigns. There's a stampede of fear. Everyone, everywhere, is asking the same question. The news media, politicians, pundits, military commanders, bloggers, and religious leaders are incessantly asking this question. It appears in many forms and is stated in different ways, but no matter who you talk to the basic question is the same: *What on earth just happened?*

The newspapers and cable television are totally unable to grasp and report the magnitude of this news. Some are saying this must be the Rapture, because they heard about it in church or read about it in a book. Others are attempting to explain it scientifically—as a massive UFO abduction, or some secret weapon that vaporizes people—but they will stumble over their own inadequacies to explain what happened. The only reliable source to find out what on earth just happened is the Bible, God's holy Word, where the vanishing of millions of people was predicted in detail by Jesus Christ and His apostles two millennia ago. I want you to understand that what has happened is not an inexplicable mystery but rather it is an amazing fulfillment of biblical prophecy. While the Rapture took the world completely by surprise, it has been anticipated and expected by Bible-believing Christians ever since Jesus returned to heaven after His death and resurrection. Make no mistake: this is the beginning of the end.

In the wake of what's happened, your mind is undoubtedly flooded with all kinds of questions about the vanishing—or what is commonly known as the Rapture. What is the Rapture? Why did it happen? Why were so many people left behind? Where did all the people go? How is the Rapture related to the Second Coming of Jesus? What now? Is it too late? Is there any hope? Those are sober questions—searching questions. And nothing is more important for you right now than understanding the implications of the Rapture because it is the catalyst for all the events that are coming upon the earth in the next few years. It is the inaugural event on God's prophetic calendar. It has set in motion a series of disastrous calamities that cannot be reversed or stopped.

So, to help you get a grasp on what has just happened, I want to begin by providing you with a simple summary of what the Bible says about the Rapture and some answers to the questions on everyone's minds.

WHAT IS THE RAPTURE?

According to my online dictionary, the word *rapture* means "an expression or manifestation of ecstasy or passion" and "being carried away by overwhelming emotion."[3] But according to the Bible, the Rapture is the event in which all who have put their trust in Jesus Christ are suddenly caught up from the earth and taken into heaven by Him. The English word *rapture* is a translation of the Greek word *harpazo*. It occurs fourteen times in the New Testament, and it means "to carry off by force," "to seize," or "to carry away."

To help you get your bearings concerning the Rapture, here are two key biblical texts that explain its major movements. Please read these words thoughtfully and carefully.

Behold, I tell you a mystery: We shall not all sleep, but we shall all be changed—in a moment, in the twinkling of an eye, at the last trumpet. For the trumpet will sound, and the dead will be raised incorruptible, and we shall be changed. For this corruptible must put on incorruption, and this mortal must put on immortality. (1 Corinthians 15:51–53)

I do not want you to be ignorant, brethren, concerning those who have fallen asleep, lest you sorrow as others who have no hope. For if we believe that Jesus died and rose again, even so God will bring with Him those who sleep in Jesus. For this we say to you by the word of the Lord, that we who are alive and remain until the coming of the Lord will by no means precede those who are asleep. For the Lord Himself will descend from heaven with a shout, with the voice of an archangel, and with the trumpet of God. And the dead in Christ will rise first. Then we who are alive and remain shall be caught up together with them in the clouds to meet the Lord in the air. And thus we shall always be with the Lord. Therefore comfort one another with these words. (1 Thessalonians 4:13–18)

By putting these passages together a stunning sequence of events becomes clear. But remember that everything described in these verses took place "in a moment, in the twinkling of an eye." You know this. It all happened in a split second. However, to help us see it more easily, the Lord slows down the film to super-slow-motion so we can see it frame by frame. Join me as we examine these five frames in more detail.

THE RETURN

The Rapture began with the coming of Jesus Christ from heaven. He did not send an angel, Moses, Elijah, or King David. Jesus Himself came to get His people just as He promised. He came with a commanding shout, the voice of the archangel, and the trumpet of God. These sounds were inaudible to those living on earth, yet they served as a clarion call to gather all believers to meet the Lord in the air. When Jesus returned at the Rapture, He remained hidden to people on earth. As you know, no one on earth saw Him. He did not come all the way to earth but remained in the air as His followers were caught up "in the clouds to meet the Lord in the air" (1 Thessalonians 4:17). The Rapture started when Jesus came from heaven to gather His people from the earth to bring them to heaven.

THE RESURRECTION

Next, the bodies of those dead believers who had accepted Jesus Christ as Savior were resurrected, reconstituted, and rejoined with their perfected spirits that Jesus brought with Him from heaven. Scripture refers to those who died as "those who are asleep" (v. 15). When Christians die, it's as if their bodies are slumbering peacefully in a place of rest, ready to be awakened. These words have great import, because they convey the Christian concept of death not as a tragic finality but as a temporary sleep. Those who were sleeping in Jesus were not left out of the Rapture. In fact, they had a prominent place when Jesus came in the skies: "We who are alive and remain until the coming of the Lord will by no means precede those who are asleep. . . . The dead in Christ will rise first" (1 Thessalonians 4:15–16). The bodies of deceased believers were the first to hear the call from heaven, rise, and meet Jesus in the air.

During the Civil War a group of soldiers had to spend a winter night without tents in an open field. During the night it snowed several inches, and at dawn the chaplain reported seeing a strange sight. The snow-covered soldiers looked like mounds of new graves, and when the bugle sounded reveille, a man immediately rose from each mound of snow, dramatically reminding the chaplain of the coming resurrection of the dead. You didn't see anything this dramatic when the Rapture occurred, but although you didn't see it, that's what happened when the bodies were resurrected and taken up to meet Jesus.

CALL OUT

Let the truth of bodily resurrection bring you comfort in the difficult days ahead. If you will put your trust in Jesus as your Savior, accepting His sacrifice for your sins, even if you die in the trying times that lie ahead, your spirit will immediately be transported into the Lord's presence. Your body will simply fall asleep, waiting for the resurrection of your glorified body at the final return of Jesus. Whatever happens, remember that death is not the end; rather, it is just a temporary separation of the soul from the body.

THE REMOVAL

A split second after the resurrection of the bodies of deceased believers, Christians who were alive when Jesus came were caught up to meet Jesus in the air in the time it takes to blink your eye. They were instantly, totally transformed—inside and out. Their spirits were perfected, and they were given new immortal, imperishable, incorruptible bodies fit for heaven. Scripture calls this change "the redemption of our body"

(Romans 8:23). In his letter to the Philippians, the apostle Paul described it as the moment when the Lord Jesus Christ will "transform our lowly body that it may be conformed to His glorious body" (Philippians 3:21). The apostle John said it this way: "We know that when He is revealed, we shall be like Him, for we shall see Him as He is" (1 John 3:2).

What are those new bodies like? Dr. Arnold Fruchtenbaum wrote:

> It is possible that information as to the nature of the new body may be gleaned from a study of the nature of the resurrected body of Jesus. . . . We know that His voice was recognized as being the same as the one He had before His death and resurrection (Jn. 20:16). Also, His physical features were recognized, though not always immediately (Jn. 20:26–29; 21:7). It was a very real body of flesh and bone and not a mere phantom body, since it was embraceable (Jn. 20:17, 27). The resurrected Messiah was able to suddenly disappear (Lk. 24:31) and go through walls (Jn. 20:19). It was a body that was able to eat food (Lk. 24:41–43).[4]

A brand-new body, like the resurrection body of Jesus, awaits every believer in Jesus Christ.

Here's a simple visual image that may help you understand what happened when the Rapture occurred. Think of the Rapture as a great magnetic process. Jesus came and hovered over the earth, and all those believers who had died and those who never died were snatched up like particles of iron, pulled right out of the population, suctioned off the planet. It happened instantly. No time to get ready. No prelude. No preliminaries. This removal of living believers and the resurrection of dead believers were part of the one event known as the Rapture.

THE REUNION

The Rapture set up a delightful series of meetings or reunions. The Bible says, "Then we who are alive and remain shall be caught up together with them in the clouds to meet the Lord in the air. And thus we shall always be with the Lord" (1 Thessalonians 4:17). This is the final stage of this beautiful sequence of events.

- Deceased believers' resurrected bodies were reunited with their spirits.
- Living believers were instantaneously "caught up" and transformed inside and out.
- Resurrected believers were reunited with living believers.
- Resurrected believers and raptured believers met the Lord in the air.

The ultimate consequence of this reunion with the Lord is that there will be no subsequent parting. For those who were raptured, their union and communion with Jesus, with one another, and with their deceased family members and friends is uninterrupted and eternal. This glorious fact alone shows us why the word *rapture* is an altogether appropriate term for this event.

WHY DID ALL THE PEOPLE VANISH?

The purpose of the Rapture was twofold. First, the Rapture ended the previous age and triggered the stunning sequence of events that will follow in the final age of human history known as the end times. The Rapture was the catalyst, the divine spark, that started the prophetic countdown to the end of time as we know it.

Second, Jesus graciously snatched living believers to heaven to rescue them from the horrific devastation that is coming in a time called the Tribulation, which is an extended time of horror, agony, and devastation like nothing ever before seen or imagined. God has fulfilled the promise He made to His disciples that all true followers of the Lord will be caught up from the earth and right into the presence of the Lord without dying before the terrible time of tribulation is unleashed. Believers were promised deliverance from the coming time of wrath (1 Thessalonians 1:10). Jesus comforted His disciples with these words:

> "Let not your heart be troubled; you believe in God, believe also in Me. In My Father's house are many mansions; if it were not so, I would have told you. I go to prepare a place for you. And if I go and prepare a place for you, I will come again and receive you to Myself; that where I am, there you may be also." (John 14:1–3)

The global evacuation of believers in Jesus has removed God's people from the disastrous effects of coming earthquakes, fire, and global chaos that will consume the earth in the years following the Rapture (more about this in the next chapter).

The final book in the Bible, the book of Revelation, tells us that Jesus is coming, how He is coming, and what condition the world will be in when He comes. The word *revelation* means "the disclosure of that which was previously hidden or unknown." In Revelation Jesus promised His followers, "Because you have kept My command to persevere, I also will keep you from the hour of trial which shall come upon the whole world" (3:10). In the Rapture, Jesus kept His promise to rescue His people from the terrible time of tribulation. Jesus kept that promise, so you can be sure He will keep all of His other promises as well.

Have you ever driven in the mountains and seen the

mountainsides covered with pine trees? They blanket the landscape for as far as you can see. God's promises are the pine trees in the mountains of Scripture. Years ago, someone added up all the promises of God in the Bible and came up with 7,487![5] It's not an exaggeration to say, "Promises are the stitching in the spine of the Bible."[6] Many of the promises are positive, declaring blessings. Some are negative, ensuring consequences. But all are sure. God is a promise-making God. God is a promise-keeping God. His people could be described as people of the promise.

> **GOD IS A PROMISE-MAKING GOD. GOD IS A PROMISE-KEEPING GOD.**

Why am I reminding you of this? Because the Rapture was a promise God kept. You are a witness. The fulfillment of that promise was eternally positive for those who were taken, but it is negative for you. Nevertheless, you can rest assured that if you turn to Jesus in faith, you can claim all the remaining positive promises God has for you. I urge you to begin to read your Bible every day. Highlight every promise. Claim them. Memorize them. Cling to them in the days ahead. They are your lifeline.

RAPTURE AND RETURN

The Rapture is phase one of the final event of the end of days that is commonly called the Second Coming of Christ. You may have heard of it. Remember that the first coming of Jesus to earth unfolded in several stages: birth, life, death, resurrection, and ascension to heaven. In the same way, the Second Coming to earth will take place in two stages or phases: the Rapture (before the beginning of the Tribulation), which has already happened, and the return (at the end of the Tribulation). These two comings of Jesus are the bookends of the end times. Think of it like this: At the Rapture, Jesus came *for* His people to escort them to heaven. At His return, He will come *with* His people, bringing them back to earth. Jesus will return to earth literally, physically, and visibly.

Since you missed the Rapture, you are now waiting for the Second Coming of Jesus back to earth. When that happens Jesus will not call people to meet Him in the air as He did at the Rapture, but will descend all the way to earth, judge His enemies, and set up His kingdom of peace and prosperity. The Rapture was invisible to people on earth, transpiring in the blink of an eye, but the return of Jesus will be visible to everyone on earth. "Behold, He is coming with clouds, and every eye will see Him" (Revelation 1:7).

We will talk much more about the return of Jesus to earth in chapter 7.

After completing his description of the Rapture in 1 Thessalonians 4, Paul wrapped up the passage with practical words of encouragement: "Therefore comfort one another with these words" (1 Thessalonians 4:18). Here the apostle was telling both the Thessalonians and believers in every age that it's not enough to passively understand what was just explained about the Rapture, Christian death, and the resurrection. Our understanding should bring us comfort and spur us toward a certain action—to "comfort one another."

We all enjoy comfort. There is nothing like lounging around on a bitter cold day under the warm covering of a goose down "comforter." It gives a deep sense of protection, warmth, and well-being. It may surprise you to know that God is a comforter. I don't know what you think of God. You may not think of Him much at all, or you may think of Him as distant, disinterested, or even distasteful.

It may surprise you to know that God is described as "the Father of mercies and God of all comfort, who comforts us in all our tribulation" (2 Corinthians 1:3–4). God wants to be your comforter in the cold that surrounds you. He wants to calm your grief and distress. How do you receive this comfort? It's as simple as drawing near to Him. His comfort is available to you right now. Why not come to Him now and crawl into His warm embrace? He won't immediately drive the cold away, but He will give you comfort and warmth you never dreamed possible. And then you can enjoy

> GOD IS THE "FATHER OF MERCIES AND GOD OF ALL COMFORT."

the blessing of spreading that comfort to others around you during this time.

Though you missed the Rapture, you are still in need of the comfort this event offers. Scripture reminds us that when believers suffer the loss of family members or dearly loved friends, we have in Paul's descriptions of Christian death and resurrection all that is needed to comfort one another in these losses. Christian death is not permanent; it is merely a sleep. The Rapture reunited Christ's followers with their loved ones and friends in heaven, and it is possible that you can look forward to Christ's return to earth at the end of the coming time of trouble when all believers die during the Tribulation will be resurrected to spend eternity with their believing family and friends.

Nineteenth-century Bible teacher A. T. Pierson made this interesting observation about these things:

It is a remarkable fact that in the New Testament, so far as I remember, it is never once said, after Christ's resurrection, that a disciple died—that is, without some qualification: Stephen fell asleep. David, after he had served his own generation by the will of God, fell asleep and was laid with his father. Peter says, "Knowing that I must shortly put off this my tabernacle as the Lord showed me." Paul says, "the time of my departure is at hand." (The figure here is taken from a vessel that, as she leaves a dock, throws the cables off the fastenings, and opens her sails to the wind to depart for the haven) . . . The only time where the word "dead" is used, it is with qualification: "the dead in Christ," "the dead which die in the Lord."[7]

As Pierson implies, Christ abolished death so completely that even the term *death* is no longer appropriate for believers. That is why Paul wrote that we should comfort one another with reminders that, for Christians, what we call death is nothing more than a temporary sleep before we are called into our uninterrupted relationship with Christ forever. The same is true for you today and in the days ahead no matter what happens. So don't despair. Don't lose hope.

THE NIGHT COMETH

Robert Murray M'Cheyne, a brilliant young Scottish preacher who died at age twenty-nine in 1843, headed many of his letters with a sketch of the setting sun accompanied by the words "The Night Cometh." This reminded him that time was marching on. The apostle John exhorted his readers to "not be ashamed before Him at His coming" (1 John 2:28). If you're reading these words after the Rapture, then you have been left behind, and the night is quickly coming. But Jesus is also coming. The Rapture was phase one, or the first stage, of the Second Coming of Christ. At the end of the Tribulation—the approaching time of darkness—Jesus will return to earth, and He is coming for all who have come to Him.

You missed the Rapture, but you can be ready for the physical return of Christ to earth by coming to Him and standing strong against the surging darkness in the days ahead.

But before Jesus comes back to earth, there are many more predicted events that must come to pass, which raises the all-important question for you—*What's next?*

At the end of each chapter, I'm going to give you a powerful, practical promise from the Bible to encourage and strengthen you, as well as a brief prayer for you to pray with me. I understand that you may never have prayed before or that this may seem strange to you. You may be unsure. But I am confident that as you continue to read this book and recite these prayers, you will grow more comfortable praying, and even look forward to it. Be assured that God loves you and cares about you, that you can pray to God anytime, and that there are no magical words to speak to Him. Pour out your heart to Him, knowing that He hears you and is eager to strengthen and sustain you even in the darkest days you may face.

YOUR PROMISE: For He Himself has said, "I will never leave you nor forsake you." So we may boldly say: "The LORD is my helper; I will not fear. What can man do to me?" (Hebrews 13:5–6)

◄•· MY PRAYER FOR YOU ·•►

Father, Your children are lost and searching for answers. They are so confused. Nothing seems to make sense anymore. The world seems to be shaking under their feet. They recognize now, like never before, that they need You, that they don't control the world or their lives—You do. Thank You for Your patience and love. And for giving us Your Word, the Bible, to guide them through these tumultuous times. Give them hope in Your promises, peace in Your presence, and rest in Your power. Don't let their despair swallow them. Please open their eyes to understand what's happening and soften their hearts to receive all You have for them. Amen.

Have you ever driven on an unfamiliar, winding, pitch-dark road in a blinding rainstorm? All you want is to be able to see beyond the edge of the headlights. To see what's ahead. If only there was some way you could know what's coming at the next bend in the road. That is how you probably feel right now. You feel like you are driving blind. You are yearning and straining to see beyond the headlights—to know, to prepare, perhaps to avoid disaster. But can you? Is it possible to see . . . what's next?

The Bible has a great deal to say about what's next after the Rapture. Dangerous, dramatic days are ahead. You can see the warning signs all around. You need to know what's coming.

2

WHAT'S NEXT?

ISAAC'S STORM IS A FASCINATING BOOK ABOUT THE HURRICANE THAT wiped out Galveston in 1900. One of the main plot lines of the book is about how everyone was convinced that a hurricane could never strike Galveston, even as a monster storm was bearing down on them. The author vividly describes how, as the streets began to flood, people went about their business as if nothing was wrong. Children played in the water, people gathered for breakfast at the local diner, and no one fled from the storm that was about to strike with all its fury.

Some didn't worry because Isaac Cline, the National Weather Service officer in Galveston, assured them it would not be a severe storm. Others simply believed that Galveston was invincible. Some thought that since they had never seen a hurricane strike Galveston, one never would. So, for a variety of reasons, people assured themselves nothing bad would happen. And as a result, more than six thousand people died one tragic September day.

Like Galveston in 1900, a storm warning has been issued by the Creator for the entire world in the end times. A tempest of judgment is metastasizing and gaining steam. It will hit with the force of a Category 5 hurricane. I wish I could tell you the opposite. I would love to tell you that everything is going to be peaceful and prosperous in the days ahead and that all will be well, but that would follow the tragic example of Isaac Cline— except much, much worse.

Some people have not and will not take this storm warning seriously because others are telling them it won't be a severe storm. They believe it will pass by quickly. Others won't believe because they think they're invincible, or they trust in humanity's power to save itself. History books and Scripture are filled with stories of people who failed to heed warnings. When Noah started building that weird-looking boat on dry land, called the ark, his neighbors probably laughed and said, "This guy is really a pessimist." The Old Testament prophet Jeremiah warned the people of Judah that unless they quit their evil lifestyle the country would fall to King Nebuchadnezzar's Babylonian army, but Jeremiah was tied in stocks, thrown in jail, and tossed down a well. Pessimism does not make one popular. In the time of Israel's kings there was a man named Micaiah, who told King Ahab he would be killed in a battle against the Syrians. Micaiah was hated for his gloomy prophecies. Were Noah, Jeremiah, and Micaiah simply negative thinkers? The flood came; Babylon conquered Judah; Ahab got an arrow through his heart.

Pessimism and optimism are irrelevant in every situation where God's Word has clearly spoken. The Bible warns, but it also graciously provides a way of escape. People can also warn us yet offer only human methods of coping in a world under crisis management. In earth's race to the finish, people are provided with God's view and bombarded with man's solutions. As time marches on, the tempo of world events will give the entire world an undeniable sense of impending crisis that will accelerate with breathtaking speed. You already sense it happening, and, like it or not, this is the time you are facing in the days ahead. The warning signs are all around you. You are now living in the end of days.

THE TIME OF TRIBULATION

This final season of human history as we know it is addressed in many places in the Bible and has many titles and designations, but it is often referred to as the Tribulation, or "Great Tribulation." The Tribulation is a brief, brutal seven-year period immediately after the Rapture filled with unprecedented horrors, upheavals, persecutions, natural disasters, massive death tolls, and political turmoil, lasting until Christ's physical return to earth. Simply yet soberly stated, the Tribulation is a time of blistering judgment and withering destruction as God pours out His judgment on rebellious humanity. As harsh as this sounds, all who accept the authority of the Bible believe in the reality of the Tribulation, and as time marches on, unfortunately, you will see these events unfold before your eyes. There will be no way to deny or diminish what is happening.

I believe the Tribulation is a natural consequence of the Rapture. The moment after the Rapture, with all believers completely removed, every vestige of spiritual and moral restraint was withdrawn. Like the sudden removal of a dam, the world is likely now becoming engulfed with evil and swamped by sin. As the Tribulation progresses, evil will result in a climax of worsening conditions. God's wrath will be unleashed toward the wicked through the signs of His coming judgment. The result will be horrific. To help you understand what's happening all around you right now and what is coming, here are three key truths about the terrible time of tribulation that the world has entered.

THE PROGRESS OF THE TRIBULATION

The Tribulation is a seven-year period described in detail in Revelation 6 through 18. I strongly encourage you to get a Bible and read those chapters. You won't understand everything you read in your first pass, but this will give you a basic understanding of the major players and events that lie ahead.

The Old Testament prophets spoke often of the time of tribulation. One of these Hebrew prophets was a man named Daniel. According to his prophecy, the Tribulation begins when the final world ruler, the Antichrist, brokers a seven-year treaty or agreement with the nation of Israel that temporarily solves the long-standing Middle East peace crisis that has plagued the world for generations. Daniel 9:27 says, "Then he [the Antichrist] shall confirm a covenant with many for one week [one week of years, or seven years]."

The nation of Israel has always been God's clock or timepiece, revealing where we are on God's prophetic calendar. The Jewish people, who were expelled from their ancient homeland for almost two thousand years beginning in the year AD 70, have been back in their land as a modern nation since 1948. That event, predicted often in the Old Testament, was a key signal that the end of the age was approaching. Since 1948 the tiny nation of Israel has been surrounded by a sea of enemies who want to wipe her off the face of the earth. Israel has often been the eye of the hurricane in global events. For decades world leaders have worked to forge a lasting peace in the Middle East. The Antichrist will finally make it happen.

The treaty forged by the rising world leader guarantees peace for Israel. As you know, all eyes are focused on the Middle East. The signing of the seven-year peace accord between Israel and the emerging world leader signals the final countdown to the end. With the stroke of the pen, the prophetic clock begins ticking toward midnight.

This peace agreement may be signed very soon after the Rapture, but there may be a time gap of several days, weeks, months, or even years between the Rapture and the signing of this treaty. Whatever the duration of the time gap, the period between the Rapture and the beginning of the Tribulation is a time of picking up the pieces after the devastation of the Rapture and further setting the stage for the final drama. All the actors will take their predicted places on the stage. But at some point after the Rapture, the seven-year covenant isnegotiated by the coming Antichrist, ushering in a false, counterfeit, temporary peace for the Middle East—a peace that will briefly include the entire world (1 Thessalonians 5:1–3). It looks like the world's dream of utopia has been realized. Even now, as you read these words, the peace treaty may have already been signed.

What is this "covenant" that the Antichrist will make with Israel? Daniel does not specify its content, but he does indicate that it will extend for seven years. During the first half of this time Israel feels at peace and secure, so the covenant must provide some guarantee for Israel's national security. Very likely the covenant will allow Israel to be at peace with her Arab neighbors. One result of the covenant is that Israel will be allowed to rebuild her temple in Jerusalem. This world ruler will succeed where . . . other world leaders have failed. He will be known as the man of peace![1]

So, for a brief time after the Rapture, in the early days of the Tribulation, after the initial chaos settles, things appear to be looking up. But don't be deceived; this is merely the calm before the storm. Speaking of this time, the apostle Paul prophesied, "For when they say, 'Peace and safety!' then sudden destruction comes upon them, as labor pains upon a pregnant woman. And they shall not escape" (1 Thessalonians 5:3). The brief period of peace comes crashing down and gives way to the time of tribulation, also known as the "day of the Lord."

GOD IS SOVEREIGN OVER ALL. NOTHING HAPPENS OUTSIDE OF HIS PLANS AND PURPOSES.

As you may be feeling hopeless right now, let me remind you of a key truth: God is sovereign over the times and seasons.

He is sovereign over all. That simply means that God is in control of everything. Nothing happens outside of His plans and purposes. Nothing takes God by surprise. Corrie ten Boom, who endured a Nazi concentration camp, said, "There is no panic in Heaven! God has no problems, only plans." In spite of how things might look, God controlled the events and time of the Rapture. He controls the sweeping, startling events of the Tribulation. He controls the rise of the final Antichrist. God is in control of the world; He is in control of *your* world. You can trust Him today with your life, whatever you might be experiencing.

During approximately the first three and a half years of the Tribulation, there will be a surge of worsening conditions, the anger of God against those who reject Him, and the unfolding of the signs of Christ's return to earth. During the last three and a half years of the Tribulation, the "lawless one"— the Antichrist—will be empowered to sit at the center of the Tribulation's evil as he personifies Satan. I must tell you the truth: this is a time of the greatest suffering and persecution the world has ever seen.

Jesus described the judgments in the Tribulation as the beginning of birth pains. Like birth pains, the contractions will get closer together and more intense as the Tribulation unfolds. No one can ever accuse Jesus of sugarcoating His forecast. He warned, "For then there will be great tribulation, such as has not been since the beginning of the world until this time, no, nor ever shall be" (Matthew 24:21). It will be the worst days the earth has ever faced—*by far*.

According to Jesus, these ten things will continue to multiply and progress as the first three and a half years of the Great Tribulation unfold.

1. Deception: "Many will come in My name, saying, 'I am the Christ,' and will deceive many." (24:5)
2. Dissension: "You will hear of wars and rumors of wars. . . . Nation will rise against nation, and kingdom against kingdom." (24:6–7)
3. Devastation: "There will be famines." (24:7)
4. Disease: "Pestilences." (24:7)
5. Disasters: "Earthquakes in various places." (24:7)
6. Death: "They will deliver you up to tribulation and kill you, and you will be hated by all nations for My name's sake." (24:9)
7. Disloyalty: "Many will be offended, will betray one another, and will hate one another." (24:10)
8. Delusion: "Many false prophets will rise up and deceive many" (24:11). It should also be noted that part of the delusion will be an increase in drug use. One of the

characteristics of the end times' false religion will be what the book of Revelation calls "sorceries" (9:21). The word John used is *pharmakia*, from which we get the word *pharmacy*. It is an ancient reference to the ingestion of drugs. The use of mind-altering substances such as narcotics and hallucinogens will be associated with false religions, doubtless with the approval of the government.

9. Defection: "Because lawlessness will abound, the love of many will grow cold" (24:12). People will turn away from God and from one another.

10. Declaration: "This gospel of the kingdom will be preached in all the world as a witness to all the nations" (24:14). In the midst of the darkness the light of the good news of Jesus Christ will shine brighter than ever. People everywhere will run to Jesus Christ for forgiveness, peace, and life.

Jesus spoke clearly about the Tribulation, but He is not alone. Several passages throughout the Bible describe the events that will occur during the Tribulation period. These descriptions occur in the writings of various Old Testament prophets and in brief references here and there in other books of the Bible. But it is the book of Revelation that describes the Tribulation events in the greatest detail.

THE PICTURE OF THE TRIBULATION

I have found that many people wonder just what the Tribulation is, or even what the word means. This perplexity gives us a good place to start. The word is little used in ordinary conversation today. Most of us are aware of it only because of its use in the Bible. *Tribulation* is translated from the Greek *thlipsis*, a term designating the giant weight used to crush grain into flour.[2] So the idea behind *tribulation* is utterly crushing, pulverizing, or grinding a substance into powder. The Tribulation will be a time of terror and trouble. Many of the modern Bible translations no longer use the term, choosing alternatives more common in today's language, such as *affliction, persecution, trouble, suffering, misery, distress,* or *oppression.* Yet, whatever specific term is used, the fact remains that the Tribulation is the period of time the world has now entered, and it is aptly named.

Let's explore what the Bible tells us about this present time of tribulation.

THE SURPRISE OF THE TRIBULATION

In his first letter to the church in Thessalonica, the apostle Paul described the event that will signal the beginning of the Tribulation period (1 Thessalonians 4:13–18). As we saw in the last chapter, we call this initiating event "the Rapture"—the moment when Christ appeared, raised the godly dead, and drew living Christians from the earth to be with Him. The next natural question for Paul's readers would have been, "When will this happen?" Paul anticipated the question and began chapter 5 with these words: "But concerning the times and the seasons, brethren, you have no need that I should write to you. For you yourselves know perfectly that the day of the Lord so comes as a thief in the night" (vv. 1–2). The "day of the Lord" is another term for the time of tribulation. Since the Rapture precedes the day of the Lord, Paul was saying that no one could know when the Rapture was going to occur any more than you can know when a thief is planning to ransack your house. No thief sends a letter announcing that he will arrive tomorrow at 2:00 a.m. We were not given the ETA of the Rapture. It came upon us unexpectedly, and the Tribulation is following immediately in its wake.

THE SEVERITY OF THE TRIBULATION

Nowhere in all Scripture will you find one word or description that says anything good about the Tribulation period (unless it is the promise that it will end after seven years). Moses called it "the day of their calamity" (Deuteronomy 32:35). Zephaniah said it was "the day of the LORD's anger" (Zephaniah 2:2). Paul referred to it as "the wrath to come" (1 Thessalonians 1:10). John called it "the hour of trial" (Revelation 3:10) and "the hour of His judgment" (14:7). Daniel described it as "a time of trouble, such as never was since there was a nation" (Daniel 12:1). According to the prophet Zephaniah,

> That day is a day of wrath,
> A day of trouble and distress,
> A day of devastation and desolation,
> A day of darkness and gloominess,
> A day of clouds and thick darkness,
> A day of trumpet and alarm
> Against the fortified cities
> And against the high towers. (Zephaniah 1:15–16)

Jesus told us that the Tribulation will be a time of terror and horror without precedent: "For then there will be great tribulation, such as has not been since the beginning of the world until this time, no, nor ever shall be. And unless those days were shortened, no flesh would be saved; but for the elect's sake those days will be shortened" (Matthew 24:21–22).

The central chapters of Revelation give us a vivid description of the horrors of the Tribulation period. Great wars ravage the world as nations rise up, lusting for conquest. All peace will end, and rampant slaughter will bloody the earth. Hail and fire will burn up the earth's grass and destroy a third of all trees. Intense famine will dry up food supplies. Rivers and seas will become too polluted to sustain life. Many rivers will dry up entirely. The sun will scorch the earth and its inhabitants like fire. A quarter of the world's population will die from war, starvation, and beastly predators. Giant earthquakes, accompanied by thunder and lightning, will destroy cities. Mountains will crash into the seas, killing a third of the fish. Tidal waves from the cataclysm will sink a third of all the world's ships. A massive meteor shower will strike the earth. Ashes and smoke rising from its devastation will hide the sun and moon. Swarms of demonic insects will darken the sun and inflict painful stings. Rampant, epidemic plagues will kill one-fourth of all mankind. Everyone, from national leaders to servants and slaves, will flee the cities to hide in caves and under rocks (Revelation 6:2–17; 8:8–13; 9:1–20; 16:1–21).

To make matters even worse, a maniacal despot known as the Antichrist will rise to power. He will be multiple times more demonic than Nero, Stalin, and Hitler combined. He will demand total allegiance to his satanically inspired program, and those who resist will be barred from buying or selling food or any other product. His lust for power will not cease until the entire civilized world chokes in his tyrannical grasp (Revelation 13:1–18).

I know this is not a pretty picture. It is not an overstatement to say that the Tribulation will be hell on earth. There will be no escape and no relief.

THE PURPOSE OF THE TRIBULATION

By now, I'm sure you are wondering, *Why is a time like the Tribulation necessary? Why is a loving God pouring out such undiluted wrath and judgment on the earth? Why have I been caught up in this terrible time?* The answer to these important questions is simple yet sobering. The Tribulation has been unleashed on the earth because of humanity's increasing rebellion and rampant sin. God's hand is heavily involved, just as it was when He brought the plagues on the rebellious nation of Egypt in the book of Exodus. The Tribulation is a planned, prophesied program and period designed to accomplish two important goals.

THE TRIBULATION PURIFIES ISRAEL

Have you ever wondered why the tiny nation of Israel is at the center of so much global diplomacy and controversy? Why is this thin sliver of land in the Middle East so sought after and fought over? The answer is simple. The Jewish nation exists as a result of God's eternal promise—His covenant—to Abraham that his descendants would be as numerous as the stars in heaven, that they would inherit the land of Israel, and that they would endure throughout all eternity (Genesis 12:1–3; 15:5). Throughout the millennia, the Jewish nation has been the recipient of God's richest blessings and the source of the Bible (God's written word) and the Messiah, Jesus Christ (God's living Word). Nevertheless, the Jewish people have tested God's patience throughout the many centuries of their existence, turning away from Him time and time again. But despite Israel's persistent rebellion, God has and will keep His promise, not only because He is God and does not break His promises but also because of His deep love for Israel. One of the final phases of His promise to Israel was fulfilled in 1948, when the nation was reestablished on its originally promised land. Yet after all God's care to preserve the scattered Jews through the centuries, enabling them to remain intact so they could inherit their land, they remain spiritually rebellious even today, spurning God's Son, Jesus Christ.

The first purpose of the Tribulation is to purge out from the Jewish people those who refuse to turn to Jesus Christ and bring about the final conversion of the Jewish nation. The Tribulation will be the fire that purifies Israel by burning out all the dross and impurities. Many wonder how the Jewish people have remained a distinct people after being out of their ancient homeland for almost two thousand years. Israel's reestablishment as a modern nation is a miracle in preparation for God's plan to restore them spiritually in the last days. As the prophet Ezekiel recorded, "I will make you pass under the rod. . . . I will purge the rebels from among you, and those who transgress against Me" (Ezekiel 20:37–38). Moses also wrote of Israel's purging in the last days and urged the nation to respond by turning back to God:

When you are in distress, and all these things come upon you
in the latter days, when you turn to the LORD your God and
obey His voice (for the LORD your God is a merciful God),
He will not forsake you nor destroy you, nor forget the covenant of your fathers which He swore to them. (Deuteronomy
4:30–31)

The apostle Paul left no ambiguity as to whether this purging prophesied by Moses and Ezekiel would be effective: "And so
all Israel will be saved, as it is written: 'The Deliverer will come
out of Zion, and He will turn away ungodliness from Jacob; for
this is My covenant with them, when I take away their sins'"
(Romans 11:26–27). Through the troubles of the time of tribulation, God will accomplish His purpose and bring a remnant of
the Jewish people to trust in Jesus as their Messiah.

THE TRIBULATION PUNISHES SINNERS

As unpalatable as it must seem to you, the overall purpose of
the Tribulation is to execute God's wrath upon those who oppose
Him—first upon the Jews who have rebelled, as we have already
shown, and then upon the rebellious Gentiles. As Scripture says,
"For the wrath of God is revealed from heaven against all ungodliness and unrighteousness of men, who suppress the truth in
unrighteousness" (Romans 1:18).

Admittedly, we like to think and speak about the love of

God, but not so much about His wrath. But wrath goes hand in hand with judgment, and it is as much an expression of God's goodness as His love. In fact, love and wrath are two sides of the same coin. One who is infinitely good, as God is, rightly abhors evil because evil is the enemy of goodness. Evil is, in fact, like a parasite, a blight, or a cancer on goodness. It feeds on and, thus, destroys good. Therefore, God rightly directs His wrath at evil.

> The biblical doctrine of God's wrath is rooted in the doctrine of God as the good, wise and loving creator, who hates—yes, hates, and hates implacably—anything that spoils, defaces, distorts, or damages this beautiful creation, and in particular anything that does that to his image-bearing creatures. If God does not hate racial prejudice, he is neither good nor loving. If God is not wrathful at child abuse, he is neither good nor loving. If God is not utterly determined to root out from his creation, in an act of proper wrath and judgment, the arrogance that allows people to exploit, bomb, bully and enslave one another, he is neither loving, nor good, nor wise.[3]

The prophet Nahum explained the nature of God's wrath in this way: "The LORD avenges and is furious. The LORD will take vengeance on His adversaries, and He reserves wrath for His enemies; the LORD is slow to anger and great in power, and will not at all acquit the wicked" (Nahum 1:2–3).

Don't lose sight of the love of God in all the suffering and wreckage you see around you. God loves you more than you can ever know or experience. How do I know God loves you? Because of what God says and what He does. He showed you His love for you by sending His Son, Jesus, to earth to take on humanity to die in your place—to die as your substitute. The Bible says, "For God so loved the world that He gave His only begotten Son, that whoever believes in Him should not perish but have everlasting life" (John 3:16). The Bible also says, "But God demonstrates His own love toward us, in that while we were still sinners, Christ died for us" (Romans 5:8). Jesus is the proof that God loves you. When you're tempted to doubt God's love for you or for His world, remember Jesus. He is the love of God on display for you to see.

> GOD SHOWED YOU HIS LOVE FOR YOU BY SENDING HIS SON, JESUS, TO EARTH TO TAKE ON HUMANITY TO DIE IN YOUR PLACE—TO DIE AS YOUR SUBSTITUTE.

To sum it up, the overall purpose of the seven-year Tribulation period is to expose unregenerate, lost people, both Jews and Gentiles, to the wrath of God. Just as the sun hardens clay and softens butter, God's wrath hardens some hearts and softens others. This shows us that the purpose of the Tribulation includes both conversion and condemnation, depending on how the objects of God's wrath respond to it. Do not allow what's happening in the world and in your own life to harden you against the Lord. Make sure the "Son" softens your heart to receive Him. He is your only hope in life and death.

HEED THE WARNING

I realize that at this point you may need to stop and catch your breath. This is a lot to take in. I know the outlook I've presented in this chapter is not pretty. It's not palatable or pleasant, but it is true. You know it's true because you can see it beginning already. A monster storm is metastasizing. Nothing can ward it off. Don't ignore the warnings. The hour hand on God's time clock is wound up and spinning. You are being swept along the path of history by a swift wind at your back. Your ability to weather the storm will come from your relationship with Jesus Christ and understanding of the Word of God.

Jesus put it plainly: There are two ways to prepare for a storm. You can build on the rock and stand or build on the sand and fall.

> "Therefore whoever hears these sayings of Mine, and does them, I will liken him to a wise man who built his house on the rock: and the rain descended, the floods came, and the winds blew and beat on that house; and it did not fall, for it

was founded on the rock. But everyone who hears these say-
ings of Mine, and does not do them, will be like a foolish man
who built his house on the sand: and the rain descended, the
floods came, and the winds blew and beat on that house; and
it fell. And great was its fall." (Matthew 7:24–27)

In 2017 Hurricane Irma pummeled the Florida coast with
ferocious Category 5 winds. In the aftermath the landscape
looked like a bomb went off. But a few houses withstood the
pounding. Which ones? Those built in keeping with the most
recent Florida building codes.[4] Houses built to code did not fall.
They weathered the storm.

The same is true for your life. Make sure to build your life
according to the divine building code. Build your life on the firm
foundation of Jesus Christ. Any other foundation will fail you
when you need it most.

You missed the Rapture, and there is nothing now you can
do to reverse that. But God, in His grace, has extended more
time for you to come to Him. As long as you are alive there is
hope. Take every advantage of His multiplied mercy, and make
sure to build your life on the solid rock of Jesus Christ so you
can stand in the storm.

YOUR PROMISE: "Now when these things begin to happen, look up and lift up your heads, because your redemption draws near." (Luke 21:28)

➤· MY PRAYER FOR YOU ·➤

Father, Your children are scared. They see the storm clouds gathering. Ominous events are beginning to unfold all around, and there's no sign it will get better, just worse and worse. They've never seen anything like this. It's worse than anyone could have ever imagined. In the Bible you've revealed information about the Tribulation and why it's necessary, but Your children are still frightened and unsettled. They need You. They need Your insight and guidance. They need Your presence. Give them the strength to trust You even when things look out of control. Cover them with Your blanket of peace. Help them trust You no matter what happens. Help them know how to allow Jesus to be the foundation of their lives. Please help them stand. Amen.

Across the millennia, planet earth has endured every kind of imaginable disaster and destruction—the explosion of Santorini in the Aegean Sea, the eruption of Mt. Vesuvius, the detonation of Krakatoa, massive tsunamis, terrifying earthquakes, overwhelming floods, raging fires, global pandemics, and ravaging hurricanes and typhoons. Disaster is nothing new for our world, but what the earth is facing in the wake of the Rapture is *literally* disaster of "biblical proportion." It's apocalypse now. Everyone knows it. Everyone sees it. The question on everyone's mind is, how bad will it get? The simple, yet sobering, answer is really, really bad. There's no way to mitigate or alleviate the magnitude of the looming disaster in any way.

3

HOW BAD WILL IT GET?

ROBERT INGERSOLL WAS A WELL-KNOWN NINETEENTH-CENTURY ATHE-ist who often delivered defiant speeches against God. In the middle of one of his atheistic rants, he pulled his watch from his pocket and said, "According to the Bible, God has struck men dead for blasphemy. I will blaspheme Him and give Him five minutes to strike me dead and damn my soul."

The crowd was hushed in silence while one minute ticked by. Two minutes passed, and you could feel the nervousness in the audience build. Three minutes passed, and a woman fainted from fear; four minutes came and went, and Ingersoll curled his lip. As the minute hand hit five minutes, he snapped his watch shut, put it in his pocket, and said, "You see, there is no God, or He would have taken me at my word and struck me dead."

The story was later related to British preacher Joseph Parker, who said, "And did the American gentleman think he could exhaust the patience of God in five minutes?" [1] I love that story because it reminds us of God's great patience and longsuffering with sinners, even hardened sinners who openly reject and blaspheme His name. Think of how patient God has been with sinful humanity throughout the millennia. Think about how patient God has been with you. I'm so thankful for the patience of God.

But despite His great patience, God does not withhold judgment forever. God is patient, but He is also holy and just. Scripture is replete with examples of God's patience running out—with individuals, families, nations, and even the entire world in the days of Noah. Jesus said the end of days would be like the days of Noah, when God flooded the earth, and once again the patience of God with this world has reached its breaking point. Patience has given way to vengeance. The time of tribulation has come.

I realize this is not an appealing subject and that this chapter is not easy reading. I fully recognize that you won't enjoy going through this chapter. But no matter how difficult this is for you, and how badly you may want to skip it, you need to know what's coming, as awful as it is. You need to know this for yourself and for others you love and care about. God has graciously provided a warning of what's coming. The most detailed description in the Bible of what lies ahead is outlined in chapters 6 through 16 of Revelation.

The main thrust in these eleven chapters is three sets of seven divine judgments that are unleashed on planet earth in devastating succession. These three series of seven judgments are identified as seven seals, seven trumpets, and seven bowls of wrath. There is no way to understand the Tribulation without making our way through these three sets of judgment.

THE FIRST SET OF JUDGMENTS— SEVEN SHOCKING SEALS

In Revelation 4–5, before the Tribulation begins, you encounter Jesus Christ poised to take back control of the earth. He approaches the throne of God and takes a scroll from the right hand of God the Father. This scroll is the title deed to the earth; it's the inheritance of the kingdoms of this world. As each of the seals of the scroll is broken, the scroll is unrolled to reveal multiple phases of God's wrath to be poured upon this wicked earth. As the scroll continues to unroll, a series of judgments falls upon a groaning planet. The seeds of disaster spread with increasing intensity. When the scroll is finally and fully opened in Revelation 19, Jesus will return to earth, take control of the planet, and establish His global reign. He will take back planet earth. He will receive the nations as His inheritance.

Let me encourage you to surrender your life to Jesus if you never have. He is Lord of all. When He returns to earth to receive the kingdoms of this world as His inheritance, every knee will bow to Him. Since all of creation is ultimately headed to the feet of Jesus, why not get a head start and begin to live there now? Every morning when you get up, fall down before Jesus and worship Him. Then, make all your decisions and live all your life in light of His lordship.

> JESUS WILL RETURN AND RECEIVE THE KINGDOMS OF THE WORLD AS HIS INHERITANCE, AND EVERY KNEE WILL BOW TO HIM.

In the sixth chapter of Revelation, the first four seals are broken to reveal the events that will initiate the seven years of trouble upon the earth—the seven years that we know as the Tribulation. As the four seals are opened, one of the four living creatures in heaven summons a rider on a horse to go forth upon the earth. These are often called the "Four Horsemen of the Apocalypse." The horses and riders are not literal; they're symbolic. But this does not mean they are not real. They point beyond the symbols to judgments that are literal. In the Bible horses often represent God's activity on earth and the forces He uses to accomplish His divine purposes (Zechariah 1:8–17).

Here's a brief snapshot of the seals. First, the white horse gallops onto the world scene carrying the man of deception, the coming world dictator; second, the red horse claws the air, abolishing any semblance of peace on earth; third, the black horse appears, creating hunger and economic disaster; fourth, the pale horse spreads deadly plague in its path. The fifth seal reveals the martyred believers who are killed during the Tribulation, and the sixth seal unleashes a devastating earthquake and cosmic signs. The seventh seal contains the next series of judgments— the seven trumpets.

These seven seal judgments compel us to examine them in more detail.

SEAL ONE: RIDER ON A WHITE HORSE

"I looked, and behold, a white horse. He who sat on it had a bow; and a crown was given to him, and he went out conquering and to conquer" (Revelation 6:2). When Rome's generals returned from war victorious, they would parade down the main thoroughfare on horses—conquerors making a grand entrance while receiving the accolades of the admiring citizens. Here also in Revelation we have a picture of a war hero who mounts a white horse. The rider is none other than the Antichrist, the emerging world dictator, who rides into the world at the beginning of the Tribulation period promising to bring peace in the midst of global turmoil.

The world after the Rapture is looking for a man on a white horse who will convince everyone that he is a man of peace. The image in Revelation 6:2 supports this peace-bringing interpretation. The crown the rider wears is one of victory, but his bow has no arrows. It is the picture of a bloodless victory gained through peaceful negotiations. In the midst of nations threatening one another with nuclear war, and terrorists becoming ever more sophisticated with their weapons, the final dictator, promising peace and prosperity, is welcomed as the savior and hope of the world. His eloquence and promises mesmerize the masses. Armies and governments are united under his leadership. The people of the earth sigh in relief.

In fact, the Antichrist will actually bring peace to the Middle East. With Israel surrounded by enemies, the person who can finally resolve these endless and previously unsolvable conflicts plaguing Israel and its Islamic neighbors will be lauded as the greatest diplomat of all time. Daniel predicted this man's arrival when he said there is a "prince who is to come," who will make a covenant with Israel to protect her from her enemies (Daniel 9:26–27). He will have the support of all the nations of the earth.

But unlike the stereotypical riders of white horses you may have seen in old Western movies, this man is not a hero. He is a wolf in sheep's clothing with no intention of keeping his promises, bringing peace, or continuing his protection of Israel. He is, in fact, by far the worst tyrant ever to appear on the face of the earth.

SEAL TWO: RIDER ON A RED HORSE

"Another horse, fiery red, went out. And it was granted to the one who sat on it to take peace from the earth, and that people should kill one another; and there was given to him a great sword" (Revelation 6:4). When Jesus removes the second seal, the angel summons the second horse. This blood-red beast is ridden by a being who carries an assassin's sword.

The rider on the red horse represents not only nation rising against nation and kingdom against kingdom, but also man fighting against man. He ushers in a time of murders, assassinations, bloodshed, and revolution that will far exceed even the worst we have seen throughout history.

The levels of conflict that civilization endures and the volume of blood that is spilled during the Tribulation—when the Rapture has removed all godly influence from the world—will be unimaginable. When the second seal is opened, this is the message:

"You will hear of wars and rumors of wars. See that you are not troubled; for all these things must come to pass, but the end is not yet. For nation will rise against nation, and kingdom against kingdom. And there will be famines, pestilences, and earthquakes in various places. All these are the beginning of sorrows. . . . For then there will be great tribulation, such as has not been since the beginning of the world until this time, no, nor ever shall be. And unless those days were shortened, no flesh would be saved; but for the elect's sake those days will be shortened." (Matthew 24:6–8, 21–22)

You may wonder how those days can be shortened and even how it's possible to survive such horror. The shortening of the time means that it will be limited to the time Scripture predicts—seven years. Mercifully, it won't run on any longer.

I realize this may all be overwhelming, perceived as overly depressing, or seen as the cries of an alarmist. Yet, despite these possible criticisms and misunderstandings, the truth needs to be told and the alarm needs to be sounded. I must alert people to this dark shadow that is already unfolding and looms ominously on the horizon. Only when you are warned can you prepare.

SEAL THREE: RIDER ON A BLACK HORSE

One of the tragic consequences of war is famine. This leads us to the breaking of the third seal:

When He opened the third seal, I heard the third living creature say, "Come and see." So I looked, and behold, a black horse, and he who sat on it had a pair of scales in his hand.

And I heard a voice in the midst of the four living creatures saying, "A quart of wheat for a denarius, and three quarts of barley for a denarius; and do not harm the oil and the wine." (Revelation 6:5–6)

In John's time a quart of wheat was the amount of food one person needed to survive each day. In the early days of the Tribulation period, this amount of food sells for the equivalent of one day's wages. Or, to put it more succinctly, the price of groceries rises so high that a person will have to work all day to buy enough food to feed one person just one meal. Runaway hyperinflation gobbles up whatever money is earned. Food shortages and widespread starvation are inevitable. Even now, the shadow of worldwide inflation and famine looms over the earth. The rider on the black horse assures you that a famine of disastrous proportions is on God's prophetic calendar during the Tribulation.

SEAL FOUR: RIDER ON A PALE HORSE

As the world experiences the devastation of the first three horsemen, John reveals the fourth rider:

When He opened the fourth seal, I heard the voice of the fourth living creature saying, "Come and see." So I looked, and behold, a pale horse. And the name of him who sat on it was Death, and Hades followed with him. And power was given to them over a fourth of the earth, to kill with sword, with hunger, with death, and by the beasts of the earth. (Revelation 6:7–8)

John then saw two persons riding out toward the earth: Death mounted on a pale horse, and Hades following closely behind. They have enormous power by which they will kill a fourth of the population of the earth. The Greek word used here to describe the color of Death's horse means "ashen" or "pale." It further describes the yellowish green color of decomposition— the pallor of the face of a corpse in the state of advanced decay.

In his book *Swindoll's Living Insights New Testament Commentary: Revelation*, Charles Swindoll describes the carnage of the rider on the pale horse this way: "In this terrifying scene John saw the grim reaper and the grave digger moving together across the face of the earth. 'Death' slays the body while 'Hades' swallows up the soul. These two figures symbolize the massive number of deaths that will follow in the wake of the first three horsemen. One-quarter of the world's population will be lost in their rampage!"[2]

God's judgments during the Tribulation are described as the "sword, and the famine, and the noisome beast, and the pestilence" (Ezekiel 14:21 KJV). History has demonstrated a close association between these four terrible forces. Deadly, global plagues and pandemics will reinforce and further the agenda of Satan and the Antichrist to support their argument for a one-world government led by a seemingly benevolent, peace-loving dictator.

SEAL FIVE: THE VOICE OF THE MARTYRS

The fifth seal is opened, revealing the painful plight of those who trust in Jesus after the Rapture. During the Tribulation, it's open season on believers in Jesus who face persecution and even death for their faith. In a world that loves to talk about tolerance, there is no tolerance for followers of Jesus.

> When He opened the fifth seal, I saw under the altar the souls of those who had been slain for the word of God and for the testimony which they held. And they cried with a loud voice, saying, "How long, O Lord, holy and true, until You judge and avenge our blood on those who dwell on the earth?" Then a white robe was given to each of them; and it was said to them that they should rest a little while longer, until both the number of their fellow servants and their brethren, who would be killed as they were, was completed. (Revelation 6:9–11)

Jesus graphically described this purge of believers. "Then they will deliver you up to tribulation and kill you, and you will be hated by all nations for My name's sake. And then many will be offended, will betray one another, and will hate one another"

(Matthew 24:9–10). The truth is, if you choose to follow Jesus Christ, you may have to give your life for your faith. But let me encourage you to stand strong. You may lose your life, but you will receive eternal life that you can never lose.

SEAL SIX: HEAVENLY SIGNS AND EARTHLY SHELTER

The sixth seal unleashes cosmic signs that increase the sense of dread and fear and grip people's hearts. It will rock the world.

> I looked when He opened the sixth seal, and behold, there was a great earthquake; and the sun became black as sackcloth of hair, and the moon became like blood. And the stars of heaven fell to the earth, as a fig tree drops its late figs when it is shaken by a mighty wind. Then the sky receded as a scroll when it is rolled up, and every mountain and island was moved out of its place. And the kings of the earth, the great men, the rich men, the commanders, the mighty men, every slave and every free man, hid themselves in the caves and in the rocks of the mountains, and said to the mountains and rocks, "Fall on us and hide us from the face of Him who sits on the throne and from the wrath of the Lamb!" (Revelation 6:12–16)

Despite all attempts to escape, there will be no place on earth to hide. God's wrath and judgment is a great leveler of mankind. The rich and powerful are not better off than the poor and powerless. They will call to the rocks and mountains, but they can't save. But there is a Rock that can save. That Rock is our Lord and Savior Jesus Christ. He's the Rock of Ages. Cry out to the Rock, and He will save you.

THE BEGINNING OF SORROWS

As bad as these first six seals are, and they are very bad, Jesus said, "All these are the beginning of sorrows" (Matthew 24:8 KJV). These are just the beginning of birth pains. This is just the first phase of the Tribulation period.

By the time the seventh seal is broken, all the accumulated horrors of the entire Tribulation period have been unleashed because in the seventh seal we see the release of the seven trumpet judgments, and in the seventh trumpet judgment we see the unfolding of the seven bowl judgments. Each seal, each trumpet, and each bowl inflict one terrible disaster after another with unrelenting regularity and intensity.

THE SECOND SET OF JUDGMENTS— SEVEN TERRIBLE TRUMPETS

TRUMPET ONE

The first trumpet sounds: hail and fire, mixed with blood, pour out of the sky, burning a third of the trees and a third of all the green grass. Blackened land, charred and smoldering, covers America, Europe, Australia, Africa, and all the continents. Wildlife dies. Death emits its acrid odors. The earth is experiencing an ecological upheaval that makes toxic dumps seem like playgrounds.

TRUMPET TWO

The second trumpet hurls "something like a great mountain" (Revelation 8:8) into the sea and turns a third of the sea to blood, killing a third of all life in the seas and oceans and destroying a third of the ships. Imagine the chaos on the cruise ships and the cargo carriers after this catastrophic event. The naval fleets of every major country will be crippled beyond help. Seafood will be rationed, restaurants will go out of business, and the source of heart-healthy food will dwindle to nothing.

TRUMPET THREE

When the third angel sounds his trumpet, a torch-like star falls from the sky, turning a third of the water into bitter-tasting liquid, which poisons all who drink it. The name of the star is Wormwood, which is a plant right out of the killing fields. The fresh water supply becomes as putrid as a Calcutta gutter.

TRUMPET FOUR

When the fourth angel sounds his trumpet, the earth becomes darkened. The sun, moon, and stars lose a third of their light. The earth is experiencing an ecological nightmare no one could have ever imagined. This fits Luke's prophecy: "There will be signs in the sun, moon and stars. On the earth, nations will be in anguish and perplexity at the roaring and tossing of the sea. People will faint from terror, apprehensive of what is coming on the world, for the heavenly bodies will be shaken" (Luke 21:25–26 NIV).

TRUMPET FIVE

As the fifth angel sounds his trumpet, a spiritual plague of demonic proportions breaks out upon the whole earth, fueled by the work of millions of demon creatures who are released from the abyss, the bottomless pit (Revelation 9:1–12). These spirits from the underworld will be hideous, but powerful, indestructible, and intelligent. What would a swarm of demons be like when released from a hell where they have been chained for thousands of years? It would be impossible to understand this whole scene apart from the vivid descriptions in Revelation 9:1–12. When the fifth trumpet sounds, Satan has his entire war corps to back him up.

Adolf Hitler, the tyrant of the Third Reich during World War II, was demon-possessed; he changed a generation and temporarily altered the course of history. What will be the result of countless thousands of demons running unchecked throughout the earth during this time of the Tribulation? It is a Dachau/

Buchenwald type of experience for those left to endure it. It is painful. "They had tails with stingers, like scorpions, and in their tails they had power to torment people for five months" (Revelation 9:10 NIV). The sting of scorpions is not lethal, but as the poison enters the system it literally sets the nerve center on fire. This torment is so painful that the agony lasts for five months. Yes, the Bible is that exact.

There are some people, however, who escape this torture. The people with the seal of God on their foreheads will be exempt. "During those days people will seek death but will not find it; they will long to die, but death will elude them" (Revelation 9:6 NIV). Imagine the agony when some attempt suicide, but find it impossible. The gun doesn't fire, the poison is ineffective, the leap from a tall building is interrupted by a net! Strange days, indeed.

Satan and demons are real. They populate the invisible spirit world that surrounds you. Knowing time is short, they are working feverishly to oppose God's work and oppose you by means of deception, temptation, accusation, and persecution. If you have received Jesus as your Savior, they have you in their crosshairs, but God has a full suit of spiritual armor for you to wear every day to

> GOD HAS A FULL SUIT OF SPIRITUAL ARMOR FOR YOU TO WEAR EVERY DAY TO OVERCOME THE STRATEGIES OF THE ENEMY AND STAND FIRM.

overcome the strategies of the enemy and stand firm. Here is the armor God has provided:

> Finally, my brethren, be strong in the Lord and in the power of His might. Put on the whole armor of God, that you may be able to stand against the wiles of the devil. . . . Therefore take up the whole armor of God, that you may be able to withstand in the evil day, and having done all, to stand. Stand therefore, having girded your waist with truth, having put on the breastplate of righteousness, and having shod your feet with the preparation of the gospel of peace; above all, taking the shield of faith with which you will be able to quench all the fiery darts of the wicked one. And take the helmet of salvation, and the sword of the Spirit, which is the word of God. (Ephesians 6:10–11, 13–17)

Suit up in your spiritual armor every day to stand against the enemy.

TRUMPET SIX

Swarming over the land as a result of the sixth trumpet is an army of two hundred million mounted troops who kill one-third of the earth's inhabitants. The pale horse of Revelation 6:8 has already killed one-fourth of the world's population. Now, one-third of the remaining inhabitants are killed. This leaves only one-half of the original number alive on the earth. Never since the days of Noah has such a substantial proportion of the earth's population come under God's righteous judgment. Some think this army of two hundred million is a force of demons, but I believe there is another possible identity of this massive army, and Revelation 16:12 gives us a clue: "The sixth angel poured out his bowl on the great river Euphrates, and its water was dried up to prepare the way for the kings from the East" (NIV). This denotes nations east of the Euphrates, which certainly includes Asian nations with massive populations. And just think, when John wrote this prophecy there were not even two hundred million people on earth.

Near the climax of the Tribulation, vast numbers of soldiers will march across the dry Euphrates riverbed. As they descend upon the scene for the last great battle of the world, a full-scale military war will wipe out a third of mankind.

GRANITE HEARTS

"The rest of mankind who were not killed by these plagues still did not repent" (Revelation 9:20 NIV). This is one of the most astounding verses in Revelation. Wouldn't you think that by this time the remaining earth survivors would fall down before God and beg for mercy? But no—their flinty eyes are hard, their mouths pursed in mockery. Nuclear war, earthquakes, plagues, deadly insects, people dying faster than babies being born—these disasters don't break the pagans.

Many factors make the Tribulation the most dreadful time in world history, but chief among them is that the Tribulation involves wrath from three sources: the wrath of man, the wrath of God, and the wrath of Satan. The earth is caught in the withering crossfire of fury from below, wrath from all around, and judgment from above. All heaven and all hell will break loose.

THE THIRD SET OF JUDGMENTS— SEVEN BRUTAL BOWLS

The final set of seven judgments are released in rapid succession in the final days just before the glorious event of the Second Coming of Jesus Christ to earth. Seven angels are the messengers who receive direct orders from God Himself, as He speaks in a loud voice from the inner temple. God's patience throughout the centuries comes to a final end. He tells the seven angels, "Go, pour out the seven bowls of God's wrath on the earth" (Revelation 16:1 NIV).

BOWL ONE: LOATHSOME SORES

This is not a pretty sight. When the first angel is commanded to pour out his bowl, "ugly, festering sores broke out on the people who had the mark of the beast and worshiped its image" (Revelation 16:2 NIV). Loathsome skin diseases are significant because they are outward signs of inward corruption.

Just reading that makes my skin crawl. The people on earth who have followed the Antichrist experience the painful fulfillment of this judgment.

BOWLS TWO AND THREE: WATER TURNED TO BLOOD

"The second angel poured out his bowl on the sea, and it turned into blood like that of a dead person, and every living thing in the sea died. The third angel poured out his bowl on the rivers and springs of water, and they became blood" (Revelation 16:3–4 NIV). I don't believe it is a coincidence that the second seal (the red horse of war), the second trumpet (a third of the sea turned into blood), and the second bowl all have to do with blood. Imagine all the saltwater fish and all the freshwater fish dying. The stench throughout the land would be oppressive. Moreover, what will people drink? The cans of soft drinks and the bottles of water and juices cannot last forever.

BOWL FOUR: INTENSE HEAT

The fourth angel gives the sun power to scorch people with fire. People will be seared by the intense heat, and many will die with curses on their burning tongues. All God has to do to make this judgment happen is remove one or two ozone layers of the atmosphere. It doesn't matter what form God uses to cause this fiery plague; it will happen. Hundreds of years before Christ, the prophet Malachi wrote: "'Surely the day is coming; it will burn like a furnace. All the arrogant and every evildoer will be stubble, and the day that is coming will set them on fire,' says the LORD Almighty" (Malachi 4:1 NIV).

BOWL FIVE: BLACKNESS IN SATAN'S KINGDOM

God centers His judgment upon the place of Satan himself. This plague brings darkness, and as people gnaw their tongues with pain from the sores and the heat, they continue to curse God and refuse to repent.

Darkness is a familiar theme in the Word of God. Many of the prophets spoke of coming darkness (Isaiah 60:2; Joel 2:2), and Jesus said that during the Tribulation "the sun will be darkened, and the moon will not give its light" (Mark 13:24 NIV).

My imagination is stretched to comprehend the horror and agony of these judgments. I can understand how you might be tempted to quit reading this chapter, but you know that this forecast is necessary and reliable because you already see it beginning.

BOWL SIX: ARMAGEDDON

Listen to the approaching cadence of this judgment that unleashes an immense army: "The sixth angel poured out his bowl on the great river Euphrates, and its water was dried up to prepare the way for the kings from the East" (Revelation 16:12 NIV). The Euphrates is the largest river in western Asia and from time immemorial has been a formidable boundary between the peoples east of it and those on the west. History frequently refers to the hindrance the Euphrates has been to military movements, but in these last days the 1,800 miles of its winding depths will be the pavement for the march to the final battlefield.

Demonic spirits are dispatched to the kings of the whole world, to gather them for the world's final great death struggle in the land of Israel at a place called Armageddon (Revelation 16:14–16). For some time I puzzled how all the earth's leaders would be provoked to fight against the armies of the Lord. The nation of Israel is such a tiny piece of real estate in the vast expanses of this world—on some maps it takes a magnifying glass to find it! Then I realized that the demonic spirits may inflame the passions of anti-Semitism until all the heads of nations are infused with hatred and seek to wipe the nation of Israel off the face of the earth.

The kings of the earth will gather in a place called Armageddon. How many times do we hear that location mentioned in modern times, and yet this is the only place where that word is found in all the Bible! The word means "Mount of Megiddo," and the valley of Megiddo is located about fifteen miles southeast of modern Haifa, Israel.

On tours to Israel I have stood many times on a steep path overlooking this fertile valley that stretches twenty miles in length and fourteen miles in width and imagined that someday the carnage there will be worse than any battle fought throughout the ages. What I imagined is quickly becoming a stark reality. A gruesome description of this devastation is given in Revelation 14:20, when we are told that blood will flow as high as horses' bridles for a distance of two hundred miles. The only valley of that length in Israel is the Jordan River valley, which goes from the Sea of Galilee through the Dead Sea and down to the Gulf of Eliat. That valley will have a red river of blood running through it.

Armageddon will not be a one-day battle; it will be a continual campaign from the time the Lord releases the deadly war machine of the red horse. Wars will rage on earth until the final battle brings it all to a deadly climax. The armies of the kings of the east prepare to attack the Antichrist, who will be in Israel at that time. This horde will cross the dried-up Euphrates to begin its death march.

Armageddon will be different from any war man has experienced in history. Supernatural events that our finite minds cannot comprehend will be taking place. Yet, earth's final death struggle will swallow up the land of Israel.

Jerusalem, the prized city of the world, which has been conquered and rebuilt numerous times throughout the centuries, is nearly one hundred miles from the initial combat zone. But this holy city will not be spared from the conflict. The prophet Zechariah said, "I will gather all the nations to Jerusalem to fight against it; the city will be captured, the houses ransacked, and the women raped. Half of the city will go into exile, but the rest of the people will not be taken from the city" (Zechariah 14:2 NIV). For centuries Jerusalem, the holy city, has seen invasions, destruction, and rape. Now it will see one last catastrophe.

BOWL SEVEN: ULTIMATE DEVASTATION

As the last bowl of judgment is tipped, it is followed by thunders, lightnings, the worst earthquake ever experienced, and hailstones weighing about one hundred pounds. The seventh angel has poured out his bowl (Revelation 16:17–21) and all the great cities fall under judgment at that time. Every city of the nations is leveled by a giant earthquake or a great shaking of the earth, which could be a nuclear exchange when the red buttons are pushed in every capital.

There will be no doubt that the end has come. The entire earth will be literally shaken, its great cities will be destroyed, and the contour of the earth will be changed. Islands will disappear; mountains will be leveled. This is the final destruction of every religious, political, and educational institution that man has built apart from God. It is the collapse of all men's hopes and dreams for earthly power.

The world is on the verge of total destruction.

The end is near!

THE END OF THE STORY

Wow! What a forecast! I'm sure you must be overwhelmed and feel like you have been drinking from a fire hose. It must be unbearable to read and even more so to live. Please know that it is very difficult and heart-wrenching for me to write these words. I love you. I take no pleasure in writing this. But remember this is God's Word. It's His unerring forecast; therefore, since I love you, it's essential that I faithfully communicate what He has predicted and that you read this, believe it, and don't lose hope.

Admiral Jim Stockdale was the highest-ranking United States military officer in the "Hanoi Hilton" prisoner-of-war camp during the height of the Vietnam War. He was tortured more than twenty times during his eight-year imprisonment from 1965 to 1973. Stockdale lived out the war with no prisoner's rights, no set release date, and no certainty as to whether he would even survive to see his family again. When asked how he made it through that harrowing time, he responded, "I never lost faith in the end of the story."[3]

May God give you that same hopeful perspective as you endure the Tribulation.

Whatever happens, "never lose faith in the end of the story." If you have come to Jesus Christ for salvation, the end of your story is better than anything you can ever imagine.

YOUR PROMISE: These are the ones who come out of the great tribulation, and washed their robes and made them white in the blood of the Lamb. Therefore they are before the throne of God, and serve Him day and night in His temple. And He who sits on the throne will dwell among them. They shall neither hunger anymore nor thirst anymore; the sun shall not strike them, nor any heat; for the Lamb who is in the midst of the throne will shepherd them and lead them to living fountains of waters. And God will wipe away every tear from their eyes. (Revelation 7:14–17)

➤• MY PRAYER FOR YOU •➤

Here is a prayer written by the Hebrew prophet Isaiah around 700 BC, to pray as you feel trapped during the Tribulation as the vice continues to tighten.

> Oh, that You would rend the heavens!
> That You would come down!
> That the mountains might shake at Your
>   presence—
> As fire burns brushwood,
> As fire causes water to boil—

To make Your name known to Your
        adversaries,
That the nations may tremble at Your
        presence!
When You did awesome things for which we
        did not look,
You came down,
The mountains shook at Your presence.
For since the beginning of the world
Men have not heard nor perceived by the ear,
Nor has the eye seen any God besides You,
Who acts for the one who waits for Him.
You meet him who rejoices and does
        righteousness,
Who remembers You in Your ways.
You are indeed angry, for we have sinned—
In these ways we continue;
And we need to be saved.

ISAIAH 64:1–5

Throughout history many people have been erroneously identified as the Antichrist. Among the candidates have been Caesars, popes, Napoleon, Mussolini, Stalin, Adolf Hitler, Mikhail Gorbachev, and even some US presidents. People have speculated endlessly and recklessly about his identity. While none of these candidates fulfilled the biblical prophecies of the Antichrist, they all previewed him in some way. But now, the previews are past. The fore-shadows are finished. The speculation is stopped. Antichrist is alive and well! He is here . . . now! And you need to know who he is, what he will do, what he will be like, where he will come from, and what will happen to him, because his reign will reach into every area of your life.

4

WHO IS THE ANTICHRIST?

THE ANTICHRIST IS THE CENTRAL HUMAN FIGURE IN THE EVENTS OF THE end times. No one else even comes close. His sinister presence will dominate the global landscape during the Tribulation. There are more than one hundred passages of Scripture that describe the Antichrist, and yet the word *antichrist* itself is mentioned in only four verses in the New Testament—each time by the apostle John (1 John 2:18, 22; 4:3; 2 John v. 7). "Little children, it is the last hour; and as you have heard that the Antichrist is coming, even now many antichrists have come, by which we know that it is the last hour" (1 John 2:18).

As the word suggests, the Antichrist is a person who is against Christ. The prefix *anti* can also mean "instead of," and both meanings apply to this coming world leader. He overtly opposes Christ and at the same time passes himself off as Christ. He is the archenemy and the ultimate opponent of Jesus. The origin, nature, and purpose of Christ and Antichrist are diametrically opposed.

The Antichrist aggressively lives up to his terrible name. He is Satan's superman, who persecutes, tortures, and kills the people of God, making Hitler, Stalin, and Mao seem weak and tame by comparison. More than twenty-five different titles are given to the Antichrist in Scripture, all of which help paint a composite picture of the most despicable person ever to walk the earth.

Some people think the Antichrist is Satan incarnate. As you witness his appearance and activities, that thought will undoubtedly enter your mind. What we do know for certain is Satan gives him his power, his throne, and his authority. Here are some of the Antichrist's aliases that give insight into his character and career:

- a "fierce" king (Daniel 8:23)
- "a master of intrigue" (Daniel 8:23 NIV)
- "the prince who is to come" (Daniel 9:26)
- "a despicable man" (Daniel 11:21 NLT)
- a "worthless shepherd" (Zechariah 11:17 NLT)

- "the one who brings destruction" (2 Thessalonians 2:3 NLT)
- "the lawless one" (2 Thessalonians 2:8)
- the "beast" (Revelation 13:1)

This list of titles reveals the infinite chasm between Christ and Antichrist.[1] As a study of these references shows, the Antichrist is introduced and described in great detail in the Bible, yet his precise identity is not revealed in Scripture. That lack of specific identification did not stop people from speculating on who he might be before the Rapture occurred. That's an indication of the extreme fascination generated by this sensational subject.

THE PERSONALITY OF THE ANTICHRIST

No, the Bible does not tell us who the Antichrist is. His name is never stated, and the second chapter of Thessalonians says that this coming world ruler is not revealed until after the Rapture of the church. But since the Rapture has occurred, this is the man you need to be on the lookout for. He is here. As you're reading these words, he may have already emerged on the world scene and you may know his name, or he may still be waiting in the wings.

But make no mistake, he is alive and ready to burst onto the global scene. Although the Bible never tells us *who* he is, it does tell us *what* he will be. Here is how he is described in the Bible.

HE IS A CHARISMATIC LEADER

The rise of the Antichrist to power makes sense. Crisis always opens the door for political strongmen to emerge with appealing solutions. The cascading crises, triggered by the Rapture, call for someone with a strong hand to take control. The Antichrist catapults on the world scene as the consummate, charismatic problem solver and peacemaker. He is the man with a plan. John Phillips describes Antichrist's rise and reception.

> The world will go delirious with delight at his manifestation. He will be the seeming answer to all its needs. He will be filled with all the fullness of Satan. Handsome, with a charming, rakish, devil-may-care personality, a genius, superbly at home in all the scientific disciplines, brave as a lion, and with an air of mystery about him to tease the imagination or to chill the blood as occasion may serve, a brilliant conversationalist in a score of tongues, a soul-captivating orator, he will be the idol of all mankind.[2]

The prophet Daniel described the Antichrist in these graphic terms: "After this I saw in the night visions, and behold, a fourth beast. . . . And there . . . were eyes like the eyes of a man, and a mouth speaking pompous words. . . . He shall speak pompous words against the Most High" (Daniel 7:7–8, 25). In these passages Daniel gave us one of the characteristics of the coming world ruler—his charismatic personality enhanced by his speaking ability, which he will use to sway the masses with spellbinding words of power and promise. We often fail to fully realize the gripping power of magnetic, compelling speaking ability. An actor who is not classically handsome can land great parts and charm audiences simply by the power of his resonant and articulate voice. Throughout history people have been swayed by political candidates who have little to offer but present it in the beautiful package of their smooth intonation and syntax. The coming world leader is renowned for this kind of eloquence, which captures the attention and admiration of the world.

Daniel went on to tell us that this golden-tongued orator not only will speak in high-blown terms but also will utter pompous words against God. The book of Revelation describes him in a similar fashion: "He was given a mouth speaking great things and blasphemies" (13:5). Considering these and other prophecies, it's not hard to understand why Hitler has often been pegged as the prototype of the Antichrist. Hitler was a man of charisma, great oratory, and pomp. In his now-classic book *Kingdoms in Conflict*, Charles Colson described the well-orchestrated events that played out in countless crowded halls as Hitler manipulated the German people.

> . . . an orchestra playing solemn, symphonic music. The orchestra stops. A hush falls over the strangely ordered crowd and thousands of people crane their necks to see. Then a stately patriotic anthem begins and from far in the back, walking slowly down the wide central aisle, comes the [Hitler]. Finally, the Fuhrer himself rises to speak. Beginning in a low, velvet voice, which makes the audience unconsciously lean forward to hear, he speaks of his love for Germany . . . and gradually his pitch increases until he reaches a screaming crescendo. But his audience does not think his rasping shouts excessive. They are screaming with him.[3]

John Phillips paints one of the most vivid portraits of the Antichrist I've ever read.

> The Antichrist will be an attractive and charismatic figure, a genius, a demon-controlled, devil-taught charmer of men. He will have answers to the horrendous problems of mankind. He will be all things to all men: a political statesman, a social lion, a financial wizard, an intellectual giant, a religious deceiver, a masterful orator, a gifted organizer. He will be Satan's masterpiece of deception, the world's false messiah.

With boundless enthusiasm the masses will follow him and readily enthrone him in their hearts as the world's savior and god.[4]

Daniel continued his description of the Antichrist by telling us he is a man "whose appearance was greater than his fellows" (Daniel 7:20). In terms of his outward appearance, this man is strikingly attractive, a handsome person. The combination of magnetic personality, speaking ability, and extreme good looks make him virtually irresistible to the masses. As he rises on the scene, people are flocking to him like flies to honey, and falling over themselves to do anything he asks.

HE IS A CUNNING LEADER

In the famous vision recorded in the seventh chapter of his book, Daniel was given a picture of this world leader. Here is what he reported: "I was considering the horns, and there was another horn, a little one, coming up among them, before whom three of the first horns were plucked out by the roots" (7:8). If we read carefully and understand the prophetic symbolism of this imagery, we see that the coming world leader rises out of a reunited, revived Roman Empire in the end times that is led by ten leaders (symbolized by horns). This will be a final Group of Ten, or G-10, that will wield great power. The Antichrist will rise from within the confines of the old Roman Empire.

Pictured as a little horn that comes up among the ten horns, the Antichrist subdues three other world leaders by plucking them out by their roots. The Antichrist will squeeze out the old to make room for the new. He will take over three nations, one by one, not by making war but by clever political manipulation. He begins as the little horn, insignificantly, but then succeeds in uprooting three of the first horns and thus appropriates their power for himself. The other members of the G-10 quickly cede all power to him. Daniel reiterated this event in the eleventh chapter of his prophecy, telling us that this future world leader "shall come in peaceably, and seize the kingdom by intrigue" (11:21). The Antichrist is a political genius, a masterful diplomat, and a clever leader.

HE IS A CRUEL LEADER

Once again, we turn to the writings of Daniel to understand the personality of this tyrant. Thus he said:

> The fourth beast shall be a fourth kingdom on earth, which shall be different from all other kingdoms, and shall devour the whole earth, trample it and break it in pieces. . . . He shall speak pompous words against the Most High, shall persecute the saints of the Most High, and shall intend to change times and law. Then the saints shall be given into his hand for a time and times and half a time. (Daniel 7:23, 25)

Here Daniel told us that the Antichrist devours the whole world; he treads the world down. He breaks it in pieces. These words hint at something utterly horrific. Many who become followers of Christ during the Tribulation are martyred for their faith. The word *persecute* in Daniel 7:25 literally means to "wear out." The same word is used to describe the wearing out of garments. The use of the word here indicates a slow, painful wearing down of the people of God—a torturous, cruel persecution reminiscent of the horrors Nero inflicted on Christians in ancient Rome, but even worse. It would be easier for the saints during the Tribulation, including you, if you were simply killed outright, but instead believers are "worn out"— mercilessly tortured by this unthinkably cruel man. Again, we find a prototype of this in the regime of Hitler. Charles Colson gives us a chilling description of what went on in Nazi concentration camps:

> The first Nazi concentration camp opened in 1933. In one camp, hundreds of Jewish prisoners survived in disease-infested barracks on little food and gruesome, backbreaking work. Each day the prisoners were marched to the compound's giant factory, where tons of human waste and garbage were distilled into alcohol to be used as a fuel additive. Even worse than the nauseating smell was the realization that they were fueling the Nazi war machine.[5]

Colson goes on to say that as the result of the humiliation and drudgery of their lives, "dozens of the prisoners went mad and ran from their work, only to be shot by the guards or electrocuted by the fence."[6] Hitler and the Nazis did not annihilate the Jews all at once; they deliberately and systematically wore down their souls. And that gives us a picture of what is happening in the Tribulation as the Antichrist is in power. I know this is a heart-wrenching description to read, but you know it is true and beginning to happen. The Antichrist is a cruel, blood-shedding leader, taking out his wrath on the believers who come to Christ under his regime. This is a horrifying picture.

THE PROFILE OF THE ANTICHRIST

In the twelfth chapter of Revelation, we read of the dragon, or Satan, being permanently thrown out of heaven in a great, cosmic war in the end times. Then in the thirteenth chapter we discover that the dragon comes to earth to begin his program by embodying his agent, the Antichrist. When we link this chapter with verses from Daniel, we get a good profile of this leader by looking at how he comes to power from several different viewpoints. Each of these angles—the political, the national, the spiritual, and the providential—give us a good picture of what he is like. So let's briefly explore what the Bible tells us about how the Antichrist comes to power.

HE BEGINS POLITICALLY INCONSPICUOUS

Daniel 7 tells us that the Antichrist does not make a big splash when he arrives on the political scene. He does not enter with a fanfare, announcing, "I am here! I will now take over!" Instead, he squeezes his way in, little by little, beginning as one among many minor political leaders. In prophetic imagery he is the little horn who grows to be the big horn. He attracts little attention as he methodically begins to grasp more and more power. John the apostle emphasized this fact when he wrote that this ominous personality arises from among the mass of ordinary people. "Then I stood on the sand of the sea. And I saw a beast rising up out of the sea, having seven heads and ten horns, and on his horns ten crowns, and on his heads a blasphemous name" (Revelation 13:1). The sea in biblical imagery stands for the general mass of humanity or, more specifically, the Gentile nations.

We find confirmation of that meaning for the sea in Revelation 17: "Then he said to me, 'The waters which you saw, where the harlot sits, are peoples, multitudes, nations, and tongues'" (v. 15). What we learn in these passages is that at first the Antichrist is not obvious. He does not burst onto the scene in all his power and glory, but rather he rises out of the sea of common humanity, emerging unremarkably from among ordinary people. But he does not remain quiet for very long.

HE EMERGES FROM A GENTILE NATION

From what nation does the coming world ruler emerge? Often, we hear that he must come from the Jewish nation. Since he will make a covenant with the nation of Israel, many people reason that perhaps he is the Jew that Israel anticipates as her messiah. But the Bible gives us no evidence for determining that the Antichrist is a Jew. In fact, we have strong evidence for believing the opposite. Dr. Thomas Ice weighed in on the ethnicity of the Antichrist:

> A widely held belief throughout the history of the church has been the notion that Antichrist will be of Jewish origin. This view is still somewhat popular in our own day. However, upon closer examination we find no real Scriptural basis for such a view. In fact, the Bible teaches just the opposite that the Antichrist will be of Gentile descent.[7]

All we know about his citizenship or national origin is that he rises from somewhere within the territory of the ancient Roman Empire.

HE IS SPIRITUALLY BLASPHEMOUS

History began with the sin of man; it ends with the man of sin. Daniel said of this world leader, "He shall speak pompous words against the Most High, shall persecute the saints of the Most High, and shall intend to change times and law" (Daniel 7:25). In his second letter to the Thessalonians, Paul described him as one "who opposes and exalts himself above all that is called God or that is worshiped, so that he sits as God in the temple of God, showing himself that he is God" (2:4). As Paul wrote in Romans 1, and as the history of ancient Israel warns us over and over, it is a terrible thing to worship a *creature* instead of the *Creator*. Yet as Daniel warned, this man defies God and demands to be worshiped instead of Him. And his demand is met. As John wrote, "All who dwell on the earth will worship him, whose names have not been written in the Book of Life of the Lamb slain from the foundation of the world" (Revelation 13:8).

As if declaring himself to be God gives him power over nature and human nature, this ruler attempts to change the moral and natural laws of the universe. That may sound farfetched, but it's been tried before. In the early days of the French Revolution, the new leaders tried to gain control of the masses by changing everything that grew out of Christianity or Christian tradition. They set up a new calendar by which years were numbered not from the birth of Christ but from the date of the revolution. They issued decrees to change all Christian churches to "temples of reason" and to melt down church bells for the metal. They actually tried to replace the seven-day week established by God with a ten-day week.[8] Such extreme actions showing hostility to everything related to God characterize the new world leader. No doubt he would even change the length of a year if he can somehow gain control of the earth's rotation!

While the Antichrist is pictured as "a beast rising up out of the *sea*," John wrote that the Beast "ascends out of the bottomless *pit*," revealing his close relationship to Satan (Revelation 13:1; 11:7, emphasis added). The Antichrist, with his seven heads, ten horns with their ten crowns, and his blasphemous mouth— whom all the world marveled at and followed—was given his power by Satan (Revelation 13:1–4).

HE IS LIMITED PROVIDENTIALLY

As you are beginning to see, the Antichrist is a terrifying person. He is the epitome of evil, the ultimate negation of everything good, the avowed enemy and despiser of God. At the same time, we must not forget that this satanic creature is not equal to God. He does not have absolute power or anything close to it. God has him on a chain. In fact, in Revelation 13, we are reminded repeatedly that the Antichrist can only do what he is *allowed* to do. Twice in this chapter, we find the little phrase, "and he was given." "And he was given a mouth speaking great things and blasphemies, and he was given authority to continue for forty-two months" (v. 5). And then, "It was granted to him to make war with the saints and to overcome them. And authority was given him over every tribe, tongue, and nation" (v. 7). Satan (and his puppet, the Antichrist) is only able to do what God allows. The Antichrist will be able to create terrible havoc and chaos, but ultimately God is still God, and no enemy of His will go beyond the boundaries He sets. No matter how bad things get or how invincible the Antichrist may appear, take comfort in the control of God, even as things seem to be spinning out of control.

One of the most comforting truths for you to understand right now is the *providence* of God. The best description of God's providence I have heard is that it is the hand of God inside the glove of human events. Epic events are swirling all around you, and it looks like the Antichrist is running things—calling all the shots. Yet rest assured there is an invisible hand—the hand of God—ruling and overruling, seeing and overseeing everything that is happening. Take comfort in knowing that no matter what you see, there is a hand you cannot see that is guiding and controlling everything.

> REST ASSURED THE HAND OF GOD IS RULING AND OVERRULING, SEEING AND OVERSEEING EVERYTHING THAT IS HAPPENING.

HE HAS AN INTIMIDATING PRESENCE

Four ancient kingdoms are depicted in Daniel's prophetic vision. They were likened to certain animals: Babylon was like a lion, Medo-Persia was like a bear, Greece was like a leopard, and Rome was like the ten-horned beast (Daniel 7). In the descriptions of the beast in Revelation, we have all these characteristics combined into one horrific creature (13:2). This likeness of the Antichrist to ferocious beasts is meant to show us the intimidating presence of this satanic creature. He combines in his person all of the threatening characteristics of the kingdoms that have gone before him. Dr. W. A. Criswell wrote:

> Think of the golden majesty of Babylon. Of the mighty ponderous massiveness of Cyrus the Persian. Think of the beauty and the elegance and the intellect of the ancient Greek world. Think of the Roman with his laws and his order and his idea of justice. All of these glories will be summed up in the majesty of this one eventual Antichrist who will be like Nebuchadnezzar, like Cyrus, like Tiglath-Pileser, like Shalmaneser, like Julius Caesar, like Caesar Augustus, like Alexander the Great, like Napoleon Bonaparte, like Frederick the Great and Charlemagne, all bound up into one.[9]

It's no wonder people follow this man and even fall down and worship him. Political campaigns throughout history show how quickly people gravitate to charisma and power. Give them a fine-looking candidate with a golden voice, a powerful presence, and the ability to enthrall people with vague rhetoric about an undefined better future, and people follow like sheep as the media bleats the candidate's praises. Completely overlooked is the substance of the man's program. The presence and charisma of the Antichrist is star power on steroids, making his continuing rise to power inevitable. He appears to be unstoppable.

THE PROGRAM OF THE ANTICHRIST

The Antichrist will rise to power on a platform of peace. One of the first acts of this world leader is to make peace with Israel as he strikes a seven-year peace accord. And he keeps this during the first three and a half years of his rule. At that point, however, he changes his tactics. He drops all pretensions of peace and adopts a program of crushing power. He breaks his covenant with Israel and subjects the Jewish people to great persecution (Daniel 9:27; Isaiah 28:18).

Then comes the leader's most sensational moment. The Antichrist is actually killed—most likely assassinated—but to the astonishment of all the world, he is raised back to life by the power of Satan in a grotesque counterfeit of the resurrection of Jesus Christ (Revelation 13:3–4). After his death and satanic resurrection, all the world responds in stunned amazement and nations quickly line up to immediately relinquish their power to him. It is then he sets himself up to be worshiped by all the people of the world. All of this transpires near the midpoint of the seven-year Tribulation as the velvet glove comes off, revealing the iron-fisted, raw, power-hungry craving of the rising global star.

The Antichrist does not rise to global power alone. He is supported by a sinister sidekick, a cunning counterpart, known as the False Prophet or beast that rises out of the earth. Through this associate, the mark of the Beast is placed upon all those who follow and worship him. Anyone who does not bear this mark is unable to buy or sell in the world's economy (more about this in the next chapter).

In a final act of rebellion against God, this vile person sets himself up in Jerusalem and desecrates the rebuilt temple in what is called the "abomination of desolation," that is, an image of himself that everyone will be forced to worship. As the embodiment of anti-Semitism, he then attempts to annihilate every Jew on earth, thus sounding the first ominous note in the prelude to the battle of Armageddon.

All the greatness of Alexander and Napoleon will be as nothing compared to him. No one will be able to stand in the way of his conquest. He crushes everything and everyone before him. He is the final great Caesar over the ultimate form of the Roman Empire. He ascends to global power ruling over one world government, one world economy, and one world religion (worship of him as God). He is Satan's CEO over a global regime. Under his leadership everything is internationalized under his personal control.

This despot of all despots is ultimately destroyed when Jesus Christ returns to earth to battle against the Antichrist and his armies. In that climactic war the Antichrist's tyrannical regime is shattered, he is cast alive into the lake of fire, and his forces are destroyed. The victorious Christ assumes His throne as rightful King and Ruler of the universe. The Antichrist will be exposed as an imposter, a pathetic poser, in the presence of the true King.

Top 10 Keys to the Antichrist's Identity

1. He is not recognized until after the Rapture of believers to heaven.
2. He begins insignificantly and then rises to world prominence as the pied piper of international peace.
3. He is a Gentile world leader from the geographical area of the Roman Empire.
4. He rules over the reunited Roman Empire (the "Unholy" Roman Empire).
5. He makes a seven-year peace covenant with Israel.

6. He is assassinated and comes back to life.
7. He breaks his treaty with Israel at the midpoint and invades the land.
8. He sits in the rebuilt temple in Jerusalem and declares himself to be God.
9. He desecrates the temple in Jerusalem by having an image of himself placed in it.
10. He rules the world politically, economically, and religiously for three and a half years.[10]

THE GOD WHO BECAME MAN

I realize the portrait I've painted in this chapter is not a pretty one. The Antichrist's reign of terror is a severe, satanic season, trapping you in its grasp, with no human means of escape. Your only answer is to turn to Jesus Christ.

Many years ago, a fictional horror film titled *The Omen* was released that portrayed the wicked life of the Antichrist. In the movie the Antichrist, named Damien, is the orphaned son of Satan and a prostitute, who died giving birth. Damien is adopted by Ambassador Robert Thorn and his wife. There is a riveting scene early in the movie that occurs in the aftermath of the nightmarish fifth birthday party for Damien. A Catholic priest named Father Brennan pays an unannounced visit to

Ambassador Thorn's office. As soon as Father Brennan is alone with Ambassador Thorn he blurts out a startling warning to the ambassador: "You must accept Christ as your Savior. You must accept him, now!"

Ambassador Thorn is stunned as the priest proceeds to tell him that his young son is the Antichrist. Thorn is infuriated and calls for security guards to escort the priest away. Father Brennan's warning to accept Christ is considered foolish by Thorn. Interestingly, however, even when Thorn finally realizes that Damien is the Antichrist, he still refuses to accept Christ.[11]

The urgent call to "accept Christ as your Savior" is more relevant and urgent today than it's ever been. "You must accept Christ as your Savior. You must accept him, now!" Don't delay any longer.

I'm sure you've noticed that many times throughout this book I urge you to receive Jesus, believe in Jesus, or accept Jesus as your Savior. I realize you may not understand exactly what that means, so let me make it as clear as I can. The forgiveness of your sins and eternal life are a free gift from God (Romans 6:23).

> **THE FORGIVENESS OF YOUR SINS AND ETERNAL LIFE ARE A FREE GIFT FROM GOD (ROMANS 6:23). JESUS PURCHASED A FULL PARDON FOR YOU. ALL YOU HAVE TO DO IS TAKE IT OR RECEIVE IT.**

There is nothing you can do to earn or deserve them (Ephesians

2:8–9). When Jesus died on the cross and rose from the dead, He purchased a full pardon for you. All you have to do is take it or receive it. When you believe in Jesus you are receiving or accepting what He accomplished for you by dying in your place. You can receive Him any time. You can do it right now. There are no magic words. God looks at the heart. The Bible puts it as simply as possible: "For 'whoever calls on the name of the LORD shall be saved'" (Romans 10:13). Call upon Him now in faith, and you will be saved from the penalty of your sins.

Antichrist takes life. Christ gives life. Antichrist is the man who would be God. Christ is the God who became man. He took on humanity to die on the cross as your substitute. He died in your place and rose from the dead on the third day. He is the Savior. He is Lord.

He will give you eternal life and forgiveness if you call upon His name in faith.

YOUR PROMISE: For "whoever calls on the name of the LORD shall be saved." (Romans 10:13)

➤• MY PRAYER FOR YOU •➤

Father, Your children see Antichrist rising just as the Bible predicts. They see more and more that Your Word is true and accurately predicts the future. As bleak as the future looks, help them to trust You. They have no other place to turn. They need You. You hold the present and the future in Your hand— and You hold everyone's present and future in Your hand. But they are still often overcome by fear over what is happening and what will happen to their families. Help them to stand strong in Your strength. They call upon You now to save them from their sins and give them hope. Amen.

No number in history is filled with more mystery and intrigue. Almost everyone, no matter how biblically illiterate, has heard about 666 or the "mark of the Beast." Speculation and sensationalism about its meaning is almost endless. It's well said that "there's been a lot of sick, sick, sick about 666." Questions abound. Is it fiction or is it fact? Is it symbolic or is it literal? Is it past or is it present? Suddenly, those questions that used to be just theory or conjecture are hitting home. The Antichrist has appeared. That means his "mark"—666—is not far behind, and with its appearance you will face the greatest decision in your life. Nothing is more important right now than for you to understand the meaning of the mark and its magnitude for your life.

5

DON'T TAKE THE MARK

JAKOB FRENKIEL GREW UP AS ONE OF SEVEN SONS IN A JEWISH FAMILY
outside Warsaw, Poland. Jakob was ten years old when Germany
declared war against Poland in 1939—old enough to remember
the German soldiers invading his town and burning down the
wooden synagogue close to his home. Like so many Jews during that time, Jakob and the other males of his family were
eventually shipped to a concentration camp. For Jakob and his
brothers, it was Auschwitz:

> At age 12, I was put in a group of men to be sent to labor
> camps. More than a year later, we were shipped to Auschwitz.
> The day after we arrived, my brother Chaim and I were lined

up with kids and old people. I asked a prisoner what was going to happen to us. He pointed to the chimneys. "Tomorrow the smoke will be from you." He said if we could get a number tattooed on our arms, we'd be put to work instead of being killed. We sneaked to the latrine, then escaped through a back door and lined up with the men getting tattoos.[1]

The Jewish Virtual Library offers an explanation for the use of tattoos:

> While it cannot be determined with absolute certainty, it seems that tattooing was implemented mainly for ease of identification whether in the case of death or escape; the practice continued until the last days of Auschwitz.[2]

As citizens of the modern world and participants in a "civilized" culture, we like to think the Holocaust represents the last time a mark will be used for identification as a way of perpetuating evil in our world on such a large scale. But it's not. Satan plans to use another mark during the Tribulation, the mark of the Beast, and its use is worldwide. I'm often asked a wide range of questions about this mark of the Beast and how it might affect the lives of those enduring the Tribulation. Here's what you need to know as you face the decision of whether to accept the mark of the Beast and the number 666 or stand firm against it. No decision you make will ever be more important. It has eternal consequences.

Revelation 13:16–18 is the biblical entry point for any discussion of the mark of the Beast: "He causes all, both small and great, rich and poor, free and slave, to receive a mark on their right hand or on their foreheads, and that no one may buy or sell except one who has the mark or the name of the beast, or the number of his name. Here is wisdom. Let him who has understanding calculate the number of the beast, for it is the number of a man: His number is 666."

THE PERSONALITIES BEHIND THE MARK

You may be surprised to learn that the mark of the Beast is not implemented personally by the Antichrist, who is described as the "beast rising up out of the sea" (Revelation 13:1). The mark is initiated by his henchman or propaganda minister described as the "beast coming up out of the earth" (Revelation 13:11) who is later identified as the False Prophet (16:13; 19:20).

The False Prophet is the Antichrist's religious leader and has the power to counterfeit the miracles of God, according to Revelation 13:13. The specific miracle mentioned in the text is the calling down of fire from heaven. The False Prophet may be trying to imitate the Old Testament prophet Elijah, when he called down fire on Mount Carmel, to make people think he *is* Elijah, who the Bible says is coming before the great and terrible day of the Lord (Malachi 4:5). He deceives people into building an image of the Antichrist as a central point of worship for the final world ruler (Revelation 13:14). With his occultic powers, he enables the image to speak (v. 15).

While the False Prophet is the implementor of the mark, he is acting on authority that comes from higher up. As Revelation tells us, "He exercises all the authority of the first beast" (13:12). And where does the first beast, the Antichrist, get his power? "The dragon [Satan] gave him his power, his throne, and great authority" (v. 2). Satan himself instigates all the terrible evil of the Tribulation period, with the Antichrist and the False Prophet acting as his diabolical agents. Satan is the ultimate energizing power behind it all.

After securing worldwide worship of the Antichrist, the False Prophet capitalizes on this success with a hostile takeover of the world's economic system. No one is allowed to participate in any financial transaction without a license, tribulation trade-mark, or passport for commerce, which will take the form of a mark placed either on one's right hand or forehead. There are no exemptions. Those who refuse the mark are barred from all buying or selling.

Revelation 13 tells us that "he causes all, both small and great, rich and poor, free and slave, to receive a mark on their right hand or on their foreheads, and that no one may buy or sell except one who has the mark or the name of the beast, or the number of his name" (vv. 16–17).

As the word *prophet* indicates, the False Prophet is a religious leader, the kind Jesus warned of when He said, "Beware of false prophets, who come to you in sheep's clothing, but inwardly they are ravenous wolves" (Matthew 7:15). Many false prophets have come and gone, but none have had the devastating impact on the world's population that the False Prophet of Revelation inflicts. He uses religion to deceive the world, and once deceived, he uses the mark of the Beast to enslave all people economically, forcing them to endure the unrelenting tyranny of Satan and the Antichrist.

THE PERIOD OF THE MARK

The moment the mark arrives is at the midpoint of the final, seven-year Tribulation period. The Antichrist begins insignificantly, rises to influence within a reunited Roman Empire, and ultimately ascends to global power. When he takes the reins of power over the whole world, the mark is instituted to subjugate the world under his authority. For the final three and a half years of the Tribulation the Antichrist rules the world economically, politically, and religiously. The global authoritarian impulse reaches its climax. Satan's desire to rule the world under the reign of one person has arrived.

THE PURPOSE OF THE MARK

Revelation 13:17 tells us how the mark functions on a day-to-day basis: "No one may buy or sell except one who has the mark or the name of the beast, or the number of his name." Only those who have the mark or the Antichrist's name or his number, identifying them as his followers, are able to sell goods and services to support themselves and secure what they need. Anyone refusing to wear the mark struggles to survive. The mark is the final piece, the masterpiece, of the Antichrist's total control over every aspect of life on earth.

It's notable that the word *mark* is translated from the Greek *charagma*, which means "a mark or stamp engraved, etched, branded, cut, imprinted."[3] The *charagma* was a symbol used somewhat like notary seals are used today. The symbol consisted of a portrait of the emperor and the year of his reign. It was required to complete commercial transactions and was stamped in wax on official documents to authenticate their validity. The word *charagma* was also "a term for the images or names of emperors on Roman coins, so it fittingly could apply to the beast's emblem put on people."[4] The mark of the Beast functions in a similar way in the Tribulation, identifying those who bear it as worshipers of the Beast and permitting them to conduct financial transactions. It could be something as simple as a tattoo or tattoo-like etching on the right hand or forehead of people all over the world.

This fusion of government and religion puts the squeeze on anyone who refuses to take the mark, leaving them nowhere to turn. Those who refuse the mark are shut out of society altogether. No one buys their products or services. Barred from employment and from shopping in stores or online, they face bankruptcy and starvation.

Given the global financial system and the acceleration of authoritarianism on every front, it's not too difficult to imagine a scenario in which people are shut out like this. But the Bible is clear that Satan's intent is not only to keep you from means of survival but also to force you to a decision: Will you continue to stand for Christ, refusing the mark despite the hardship promised? Or will you succumb to the loyalty demands of Satan and take on the mark to relieve that hardship? The choice is monumental.

Throughout the centuries, many believers have courageously faced persecution and stared into the face of death because of their stand for Christ, just as you will have to do if you refuse the mark. But during the Great Tribulation the scope of persecution is global. Pressing, life-and-death questions are put before the entire world's population, including you, without exception. They come in the form of the offered mark, supposedly to promote a good life, but with the intent to make clear who will live for Christ and who will yield to Satan. The choice could not be more consequential.

THE PERPLEXITY ABOUT THE MARK

It's not unusual for people who have never read the Bible or heard a sermon to know something about the mark of the Beast and its associated number, 666. The mark and number have been featured in novels and films, invoking mystery and terror, but usually with little to no solid biblical context.

In fact, before the Rapture, some TV and film scripts made jokes about the mark, as if Satan's work can ever be a laughing matter. This exposure is enough to make people wary of the number 666. For example, in the same way many high-rise building owners refuse to designate a floor number thirteen, many people try to eliminate the 666 sequence from their phone numbers, home addresses, license-plate numbers, and almost any other personal number you can think of. Maybe you have done that as well; the number itself can be unsettling.

Before the Rapture, no one knew what form the mark of the Beast would take, but after the Rapture the exact meaning of the mark has become all too clear. It is no longer the butt of jokes or wild speculation. The Bible gives us a mysterious clue that has tantalized theologians for centuries: "Here is wisdom. Let him who has understanding calculate the number of the beast, for it is the number of a man: His number is 666" (Revelation 13:18). Theories about the meaning of the number 666 have run rampant since the first century, ranging from the ridiculous to the absurd. No coincidence or fact from the Bible or from history is safe from becoming fodder for speculation. For example, Goliath stood six cubits high; the head of his spear weighed six hundred shekels; and he wore six items of armor (1 Samuel 17:4–7). Is the Antichrist another Goliath? The statue of Nebuchadnezzar stood sixty cubits high, six cubits wide, and six musical instruments summoned the Babylonians to worship it (Daniel 3:1, 15 NIV). Is the Antichrist a revived Babylonian emperor? Numbers in names and calendars have been manipulated to designate the pope, Hitler, and many US presidents as the Antichrist. But these interpretations were nothing more than reckless contrivances.

But now, with the Rapture in the rearview mirror, the real meaning of 666 is coming into clearer focus as each day passes, and it's less sensational than most imagined. Those of us living during the Tribulation are told "Here is wisdom. Let him that hath understanding count the number of the beast" (Revelation 13:18 KJV). The mark of the Beast is a number that can be counted or calculated. God wants you to know this number and calculate it to identify the Antichrist. Two important clues help us understand the meaning of the mark. The number 666 is identified as the number of a man and the number of his name. Let's examine these two clues.

First, John told us that 666 is the number of a man, that is, this number refers to humanity in general. The Bible often connects the number six with mankind. Humans were created on the sixth day. We are called to work six days a week. Hebrew slavery was limited to six years.

By contrast, the number associated with God is seven. Seven is often called a perfect number, while six is an incomplete number. When you try to indicate the fraction two-thirds decimally, your calculator strings out an endless succession of sixes, never quite completing a precise rendition of two-thirds. This may indicate the significance of 666. It is the number of humanity, and no matter how many sixes you add, it never reaches the perfection of seven—God's number. Man without God is always incomplete, and we long for the completeness we can find only in relationship with Him.

We all seem to have a built-in desire for completeness. We see this desire at work in a story about a trick the mischievous children of the composer Johann Sebastian Bach sometimes played on their father. According to legend, shortly after he went upstairs to bed, the children would sneak to the parlor harpsichord and play all the notes of the scale except the last one. Bach, freshly snuggled into his bed, could not stand hearing the incomplete scale lingering in his mind. He had to rise, don his robe, descend the stairs, and strike that final, scale-completing key.

Our very nature longs for completion, not only of the musical scale but also of ourselves. The number 666 should remind humanity that since the fall of mankind, something has been missing from our lives. That "something" is found in a Someone—Christ Himself, the perfect number who can give us the completeness we lack.

Second, the apostle John said 666 is the number of the Antichrist's name, that is, the numerical value of his name. This refers to something known as *gematria*, which refers to the numerical value of letters of the alphabet. Both Hebrew and Greek, the two original languages of the Bible, assign numerical value to the numbers of their alphabet. When those numerical values are assigned to the letters in a particular word, a number is derived. A number can be counted or calculated. Applied to the Antichrist this means that when the letters of the Antichrist's name are assigned a numerical value and totaled, the number will equal 666. Before the Rapture, people often tried to figure out if some world leader's name equaled 666 to identify him as the Antichrist, but that was jumping the gun. The Antichrist is revealed after the Rapture, and he can be identified both by his actions that correspond to the prophecies of Scripture and by calculating the number of his name. The numbers do not lie. His identity is no longer a mystery. His name equals 666, which means those who take his mark are literally taking his name on them. From that point on he owns them. They have literally sold their soul to the devil.

THE PRECURSORS TO THE MARK

What can make it possible for the False Prophet to effectively weaponize the mark of the Beast? Technology. Living in the first century, the apostle John, who wrote the book of Revelation, would likely have understood the mark to be like a tattoo or a brand on the skin. The possibility of using the microchip or other technologies we have today would have been an unfathomable mystery to him. But these technologies have advanced at warp speed, and the technology for implementing the mark of the Beast is fully developed and easily realizable in the time of tribulation. We also know that the mark of the Beast is fully employed in the middle of the seven-year Tribulation period.

Therefore, the extreme hardship caused by the mark could be less than a mere three and a half years away from the time you are reading this book or could already be in place, making it a very real and present danger for you and the rest of the world's present population. This is no longer a distant prophecy; it's current reality.

As I write this, I have no idea exactly how technology might be employed to implement the coming mark of the Beast. But present technology already indicates a couple of ways by which it could happen. The first is through microchips and sensors. The practice of implanting microchips in humans is growing because people are attracted to the benefits of ease and safety they provide. Microchips can be implanted invisibly under the skin. They can be read via short-range frequency identification (RFID) signals to enable the wearer to buy goods in stores without using a plastic card or cell phone. Microchips can also be used to identify everyone who walks through a security checkpoint. But there is a massive downside. Think what the Beast and his conspirators are capable of doing with access to this kind of technology and information.

Yet despite the serious and obvious downsides, more and more people are willing to surrender personal rights and privacy to take advantage of their perceived convenience and benefits. With the combination of cell-phone technology and in-store scanners, shoppers' accounts are automatically debited electronically as they carry goods out of the store.

With the mark in full swing, store scanners reading data from shoppers' implanted microchips or cell phones either allow or disallow the purchase as they attempt to buy food or other necessities. If they don't have the mark of approval, if they've refused to worship the Antichrist and acquiesce to the system put into place by the False Prophet, they'll go without. They'll be locked out of the economy. They will starve. Their families will starve. They will be rounded up and killed.

Another possible precursor to the mark of the Beast is Bitcoin or similar cryptocurrencies. Bitcoin is completely virtual money not issued or controlled by a centralized government. Physical coins and currency are completely eliminated, and all money is electronic, tracked either by implanted chips or on the internet. Some believe Bitcoin and other cryptocurrencies could pave the way for the mark of the Beast.

How, or if, these particular technologies will be used to implement the mark is mere speculation at this point in time as I'm writing this book, but it is all coming clear before your eyes. The False Prophet might use either one of these technologies, a combination of both, or some technology yet to be invented. Those who read this book years after its publication date may well experience technologies far more sophisticated than anything imaginable today. You won't know for certain how the mark of the Beast will be incorporated until it's too late to be part of the Rapture, and tragically, that's where you find yourself now. The issue now is clear. The mark is here. Will you, or won't you?

THE PRESSURE OF THE MARK

The form and nature of the mark remains a mystery until it is actually implemented at the midpoint of the seven-year Tribulation. But there is no mystery about the future of those who accept the mark. As long as the Antichrist maintains control, all will be well with those who accept it. But their time of prosperity will be short, followed swiftly by the inevitable judgment of God.

> If anyone worships the beast and his image, and receives his mark on his forehead or on his hand, he himself shall also drink of the wine of the wrath of God, which is poured out full strength into the cup of His indignation. He shall be tormented with fire and brimstone in the presence of the holy angels and in the presence of the Lamb. And the smoke of their torment ascends forever and ever; and they have no rest day or night, who worship the beast and his image, and whoever receives the mark of his name. (Revelation 14:9–11)

Followers of Christ who refuse the mark experience a complete inversion of the fate of those who receive it. While the Antichrist maintains control, they experience deadly persecution and martyrdom (Revelation 20:4). But after that, John told us:

And I saw thrones, and they sat on them, and judgment was committed to them. Then I saw the souls of those who had been beheaded for their witness to Jesus and for the word of God, who had not worshiped the beast or his image, and had not received his mark on their foreheads or on their hands. And they lived and reigned with Christ for a thousand years. (Revelation 20:4)

Followers of Jesus who reject the mark will be acting on the admonition of Christ, who said, "And do not fear those who kill the body but cannot kill the soul. But rather fear Him who is able to destroy both soul and body in hell" (Matthew 10:28).

I pray that you can take comfort from the fact that believers have courageously suffered for their faith throughout history. What is happening to you is nothing new, but it is unparalleled in its scope and severity.

- The Roman emperors Nero and Domitian executed countless Christians who refused to renounce their faith.
- The second-century Christian bishop Polycarp was burned at the stake for refusing to bow to Caesar.
- Roman Christians were fed to lions.
- Christians in medieval Spain suffered the Inquisition.
- Many Protestants of the Reformation era were massacred or exiled.

- Twentieth-century Christians in Communist Russia endured Siberia and slave labor camps.
- Even in the "enlightened" twenty-first century, before the Tribulation began, there was an alarming increase of Christian persecution and martyrdom throughout the world.

I hope you can see that you stand at the end of a long line of those who have suffered and died for their faith in Jesus Christ. You are not alone. Jesus foresaw the terrible suffering of the Tribulation period with you in mind: "Then they will deliver you up to tribulation and kill you, and you will be hated by all nations for My name's sake. And then many will be offended, will betray one another, and will hate one another" (Matthew 24:9–10).

The book of Revelation presents the Tribulation period as a time when every faithful Christian must stare martyrdom in the face. As Bible scholar Richard Bauckham explains, "It is not a literal prediction that every faithful Christian will in fact be put to death. But it does require that every faithful Christian must be prepared to die."[5]

Tragically, martyrdom is now an everyday occurrence, and my heart breaks for you. If you have trusted Jesus and stand for Him, your fellow believers, friends, and those you attend church with are suffering daunting persecution. Yet, even in the face of certain death, you are witnessing other believers proclaiming that they love God more than their own lives. Speaking of believers living during this time, Scripture says, "they did not love their lives to the death" (Revelation 12:11). I pray that God will give you the boldness and courage to follow in their footsteps and that you are willing to remain loyal to Him even in the face of death.

GOD WILL GIVE YOU THE BOLDNESS AND COURAGE TO CHOOSE THE PATH THAT LEADS TO HIM IF YOU REMAIN LOYAL TO HIM NO MATTER WHAT.

We find an inspiring example of the attitude of martyrs in a famous incident involving three young, godly Jewish men—Shadrach, Meshach, and Abed-Nego—during Judah's Babylonian captivity. When told they must either bow to the king's golden image or be cast into a furnace of fire, their response was unequivocal: "If that is the case, our God whom we serve is able to deliver us from the burning fiery furnace, and He will deliver us from your hand, O king. But if not, let it be known to you, O king, that we do not serve your gods, nor will we worship the gold image which you have set up" (Daniel 3:17–18).

You face a colossal choice. You must choose. There's no getting around this. Will you follow Christ and be marked as God's own in your heart and in your actions? Or will you be marked as Satan's own? Will you stand for Christ, His Son, no matter the personal cost, or will you fall for the Antichrist? Will you take the mark or trust the Messiah? Will you endure any hardship or persecution for His sake? When you are forced to choose between standing with God by rejecting the mark or taking it to ensure the immediate safety and security of your family, which will you choose?

Like Shadrach, Meshach, and Abed-Nego, you must refuse the safe and easy path and choose to stand for God rather than bow to evil. It's not easy. It never has been. But God has not changed. The God of Shadrach, Meshach, and Abed-Nego is your God if you have trusted in Jesus Christ. He will stand by your side just as He stood with them in the fire.

I want to encourage you to obey God no matter what and leave the results and outcome with Him. Daniel, whom I have referred to many times in this book, defied a king's command that no one pray to anyone but him for thirty days (Daniel 6). For his disobedience to the king, Daniel was thrown into a den of lions, where he was supernaturally protected by God from harm. Of course, Daniel had no idea that God would step in to supernaturally deliver him. He was ready to be eaten by lions rather than compromise his allegiance to the one true God. In your present crisis be a Daniel. Obey God. He may choose to deliver you supernaturally or may choose to allow you to be martyred to usher you into His presence. Either way, you win. And either way, God wins.

We often tend to make right choices much too complex. When the outcome seems doubtful or ominous, we want to hold off the decision while we weigh all the factors, examine all the nuances, and consider all the outcomes. But in essence, almost all moral decisions are starkly simple: either we stand for God, or we fall for Satan. Whether the result will be inconvenient or painful or even fatal should never be a factor. The only decision to be made is whether you are on God's side, which means you will follow Him regardless of the cost. Taking God's side will bring down the wrath of Satan and the Antichrist, but it will also call down the grace and mercy of God. No matter what happens, remember God loves you, and He will give you the grace and grit to face the wrath of the Antichrist as He has done for a host of faithful martyrs down through the centuries.

> OBEY GOD. HE MAY CHOOSE TO DELIVER YOU SUPERNATURALLY OR MAY CHOOSE TO ALLOW YOU TO BE MARTYRED TO USHER YOU INTO HIS PRESENCE. EITHER WAY, YOU WIN. AND EITHER WAY, GOD WINS.

The monumental decision to reject the Antichrist and receive Christ certainly means repression and loss of freedom. It probably means death, even by beheading. But remember that is how John the Baptist and the apostle Paul died. However, if you stand tall and true to God while all others are taking the mark and bowing to the image, you can rely on His promise that you will ultimately reign with Him (2 Timothy 2:12; Revelation 20:6). Cling to Him and that hope. Whatever it costs you to follow Him will be worth it. Whatever you lose in this life will pale in comparison to what you will receive in the life to come.

As you stare suffering and persecution in the face, pastor Tim Chester reminds you:

- Your suffering and your shame are for a moment. Your reward is forever.
- The area in which you now live is for a moment. The location where you spend eternity is forever.
- Temptations are for a moment. Hell is forever.
- Your home now is for a moment. Your home in your heavenly Father's house is forever.[6]

John Hooper was persecuted and faced martyrdom at the hand of Mary Tudor, known as "Bloody Mary." He was urged by a friend to renounce his faith in Christ. His friend said, "Life is sweet, death is bitter." Hooper replied, "Eternal life is more sweet, eternal death is more bitter."[7]

Let those words echo in your heart as you face the fury of the Antichrist.

Dietrich Bonhoeffer, who was killed by the Nazis, preached a sermon based on Revelation 14 titled "Learning to Die." In the sermon he said, "Do not fear the coming day, do not fear other people, do not fear power or might, even if they are able to deprive you of property and life; do not fear the great ones of this world, do not even fear yourselves."

Bonhoeffer urged his listeners to cling to Jesus to the very end. He closed his message with these words: "To die in Christ— that this be granted us, that our last hour be not a weak hour, that we die as confessors of Christ, whether old or young, whether quickly or after longsuffering, whether seized and laid hold of by the lord of Babylon. . . .That is our prayer today, that our last word might only be: Christ."[8]

That's my prayer for you. That your last hour may not be a weak hour. That your last word only be *Christ*.

YOUR PROMISE: Then I heard a loud voice saying in heaven, "Now salvation, and strength, and the kingdom of our God, and the power of His Christ have come. . . . And they overcame him by the blood of the Lamb and by the word of their testimony, and they did not love their lives to the death." (Revelation 12:10–11)

➤• MY PRAYER FOR YOU •➤

Father, Your children need Your help like never before. The choice they face is crushing. Facing hunger and ultimately death is overwhelming for them, but even more so for the ones they love. Make Yourself more real to them than anything in this world. Continue to open their eyes to all the deception swirling around them, and don't allow them to be sucked in. Help them to see the unseen and the eternal. Like Shadrach, Meshach, and Abed-Nego, and Daniel, help them to stand firm whatever the cost. Give them the strength to face whatever comes, knowing they have an eternal inheritance that can never fade away. Amen.

As a pastor, I've often counseled people who wonder if it's too late for them to receive God's grace and forgiveness. This question is usually accompanied by deep emotional pain and fear. There are many reasons people struggle with this question. Maybe they have committed some especially heinous sin and wonder if God can really forgive them. Or maybe they are advanced in years and wonder if opportunity has passed them by. The reasons for this feeling are very personal. But with the occurrence of the Rapture, I'm sure the number of people asking this question has increased exponentially. You, and millions of others, have tossed and turned at night thinking about all that's happened and wondered if there's any hope—if it's too late for you. I can only imagine how frightened and desperate you must feel. So, let me reassure you, there's still time. It is true that the window of opportunity is quickly closing, but it's not too late . . . yet!

6

IS IT TOO LATE?

ON DECEMBER 17, 1927, WHILE SURFACING OFF THE COAST OF Massachusetts, the USS S-4 submarine was accidentally rammed and sunk by a Coast Guard destroyer. The sub sunk to the ocean floor off Cape Cod with forty crew members on board. Rescue operations were quickly initiated. The surviving sailors trapped in the torpedo room exchanged a series of messages with the rescue group by tapping on the hull of the sunken sub. As the available oxygen was quickly expiring, the sailors sent a desperate Morse code message: "Is there any hope?"[1]

Is there any hope? That's a message you could be tapping out right now. It may seem like your oxygen is about to run out. You know it's true. You feel it every moment. You need hope. You need hope that God loves you and will forgive you. You need hope that missing the Rapture hasn't ended the opportunity for you to be saved and have a real relationship with God. You need hope beyond this life.

Let's get very real and honest. You are in the position you are now because you failed to receive Jesus Christ as your Savior before the Rapture. You were left behind because you neglected God's gracious offer of salvation through Jesus Christ. That's the *very* bad news. I take no pleasure in reminding you of this. But the *very* good news is—you still have hope. Enduring the Tribulation is terrible, and I'm not diminishing that, but spending eternity in hell separated from God and everything that's good is infinitely worse. At this point, you have no choice about being in the Tribulation, but you still have a choice about your eternal destination.

God loves you and wants you to know that it's not too late to be saved—that you have a future and an eternal hope if you will change your mind about Jesus and turn your heart toward Him. What God offers is not the false hope this world offers but firm hope—real hope to strengthen you to keep going.

Hope has been aptly called oxygen for the soul. Thankfully, the Bible is an oxygen-breathing book. It exhales hope that you can be saved and forgiven after the Rapture. The book of Revelation reveals that there is great revival in the Great Tribulation. Even in the darkest time of human history, Jesus is still seeking and saving those who are lost. That's the best news you could ever imagine.

Here's some of what the Bible has to say to you about your

opportunity to be saved during the Tribulation. Nothing is more important for you to hear right now. Please read this chapter slowly, thoughtfully, and prayerfully.

Your eternity depends on it. There is hope.

HOW WILL YOU HEAR THE GOSPEL?

Sometimes the most unexpected people accomplish the most out-standing feats. Dean Hess was such a person. As the newly ordained pastor of a church in Cleveland, Ohio, Hess expected to spend his life in Christian ministry. But when the Japanese attacked Pearl Harbor in 1941, he left his pastorate to join the Aviation Cadet Program, explaining to his stunned congregation, "If we believe our cause is just and necessary, how in all conscience can I ask others to protect it—and me—while I keep clean of the gory mess of war?" Hess flew sixty-three combat missions in France. After the war Hess returned to civilian life. But he was recalled to active duty at the outbreak of the Korean War to command a training program for Korean fighter pilots, in addition to flying more com-bat missions. During that time, Hess felt a keen burden for the large number of Korean children who had been orphaned by the war. He joined forces with Chaplain Russell L. Blaisdell to provide food and shelter for hundreds of children, first on a military air-base and then in a makeshift orphanage in Seoul.

Shortly after the orphanage was established, however, the Communist army marched on Seoul, forcing thousands to evacuate the city. Hess and Blaisdell devised a plan to transfer the children to a permanent orphanage on Jeju Island. Military command blocked these arrangements at first, but Hess and Blaisdell persisted until sixteen C-54 transports were approved for the mission.[2] All told, those airlifts and subsequent arrangements for food and supplies for the orphanage saved the lives of more than a thousand Korean orphans.[3]

The heroic acts of Col. Dean Hess required extraordinary courage and determination. In that same spirit the apostle John told of a group of heroes who will save millions of people in the coming Tribulation period. This period could well be called the era of the Antichrist. During this terrible time, as you know, his power is virtually absolute. He controls the world's economy and religion, exalting himself with an enormous statue erected in the new Jewish temple in Jerusalem. He ruthlessly annihilates all who refuse to bow to him.

You may not feel very hopeful right now. I understand why. But I want to remind you that God is a God of hope. The Bible is a book of hope. The word *hope* occurs more than four hundred times in the Bible. We often use the word *hope* in terms of something we wish will happen but don't necessarily expect to happen. When the Bible speaks of hope it means "desire with expectancy." Hope is something we want to happen, and we fully expect to happen. While many of your hopes may seem dashed and lost in the wake of all that's happening, God has a hope-filled future waiting for you in Jesus Christ. You can expect it because God has promised it, and you should desire it because it is the greatest reality you can ever imagine.

GOD HAS A HOPE-FILLED FUTURE WAITING FOR YOU IN JESUS CHRIST. YOU CAN EXPECT IT BECAUSE GOD HAS PROMISED IT, AND YOU SHOULD DESIRE IT BECAUSE IT IS THE GREATEST REALITY YOU CAN EVER IMAGINE.

THE PREACHING OF THE 144,000

While the unprecedented cruelty of the Antichrist increases, God does not forget about humanity. In the depths of the Tribulation horrors, the world is witnessing the greatest spiritual awakening ever to occur on planet earth. Our loving and creative God continually surprises us with the methods He devises to reach people in their darkest hours. During this time, one instrument through which His care rises is the agency of 144,000 specially chosen Jewish evangelists. We find them described in the book of Revelation.

> After these things I saw four angels standing at the four corners of the earth, holding the four winds of the earth, that the wind should not blow on the earth, on the sea, or on any tree. Then I saw another angel ascending from the east, having the

seal of the living God. And he cried with a loud voice to the four angels to whom it was granted to harm the earth and the sea, saying, "Do not harm the earth, the sea, or the trees till we have sealed the servants of our God on their foreheads." And I heard the number of those who were sealed. One hundred and forty-four thousand of all the tribes of the children of Israel were sealed. (7:1–4)

Twelve thousand witnesses will be called out of each of the twelve tribes of Israel, bringing their total to 144,000 (Revelation 7:4–8). Each of the twelve tribes are mentioned. The number twelve here is significant, for it is repeatedly connected with the nation of Israel. The breastplate of the Jewish high priest was set with twelve precious stones; the tabernacle table of showbread bore twelve holy loaves; the city of God will have twelve gates. In each of these cases, the number twelve symbolizes Israel's twelve tribes. The consistent use of the number twelve in connection with Israel climaxes in the sealing of 144,000 individuals—twelve times twelve—chosen from the nation of Israel for a special ministry during the darkest period in earth's history.

God has chosen and uses 144,000 Jews for a very special earth-to-heaven mission in the Tribulation. The powerful preaching of this Jewish army of evangelists is inspiring others with tremendous courage. After all, only twelve Jews (Jesus' twelve disciples) turned the first century upside down. You are now seeing what twelve thousand times twelve can do!

Why are the 144,000 sealed by God? As we see the judgments of the Tribulation period becoming more and more severe and the hatred of the Antichrist and his followers increasing, doesn't it make sense that God would protect His own until their work is finished? Just as the three Hebrew children were kept alive in the fire, so these sealed Jews are protected throughout the last seven years before the return of Christ. God sends them for a powerful task: these Jews preach the gospel in such a way that multitudes believe.

They are kept from harm during the Tribulation so that they might be alive until the return of Jesus and reign with Him in His coming kingdom on the earth, thus fulfilling God's covenant promises to the Jewish people. The salvation of these 144,000 and their ministry to the world is a strong dose of hope that God has not forgotten you.

How many souls are being saved by the message of these evangelists? We have a picture of the result of the 144,000 witnesses' ministry.

> After these things I looked, and behold, a great multitude which no one could number, of all nations, tribes, peoples, and tongues, standing before the throne and before the Lamb, clothed with white robes, with palm branches in their

hands. . . . Then one of the elders answered, saying to me, "Who are these arrayed in white robes, and where did they come from?" And I said to him, "Sir, you know." So he said to me, "These are the ones who come out of the great tribulation, and washed their robes and made them white in the blood of the Lamb." (Revelation 7:9, 13–14)

An unprecedented revival breaks out after the Rapture, when the 144,000 Jewish witnesses evangelize the world during the Tribulation period. The calamitous events of this period are shaking millions out of their complacency, shattering their resistance to the message of the 144,000 as they blanket the world with the gospel. Maybe you are one of those who has heard the message of these evangelists and are being shaken out of your complacency and turning to Jesus. I hope so.

The astonishing success of their final campaign fulfills this prophecy of Jesus: "This gospel of the kingdom will be preached in all the world as a witness to all the nations, and then the end will come" (Matthew 24:14).

THE PROCLAMATION OF ANGELS

A second means God will use to announce the good news of the gospel to the lost world during the Tribulation is angels. That's right—angels. The mercy and love of God is so vast that He commissions angels to proclaim the message of His saving grace. He makes sure everyone has the opportunity to hear the good news. Even the Antichrist's stranglehold on the world is not able to prevent the gospel message from going forth. God will bypass his tyranny and announce it from the heavens.

> Then I saw another angel flying in the midst of heaven, having the everlasting gospel to preach to those who dwell on the earth—to every nation, tribe, tongue, and people—saying with a loud voice, "Fear God and give glory to Him, for the hour of His judgment has come; and worship Him who made heaven and earth, the sea and springs of water." . . . Here is the patience of the saints; here are those who keep the commandments of God and the faith of Jesus. (Revelation 14:6–7, 12)

The everlasting gospel of fear of God and faith in Jesus is broadcast to the entire world not by radio, television, or podcast but by angelic preachers. That's astounding, and it's a window into the heart of God. Try as he will, the Antichrist will not be able to thwart the spread of the gospel. God will make sure everyone on earth during the Tribulation hears the good news and has a chance to respond.

When Jesus was alive and walking on earth, He stated clearly why He came to earth. "For the Son of Man has come to seek and to save that which was lost" (Luke 19:10). Jesus has not changed. Time has not diminished His love or decreased

TIME HAS NOT DIMINISHED JESUS' LOVE OR DECREASED HIS DESIRE TO SEEK OUT THOSE WHO ARE LOST AND WHO WILL TURN TO HIM TO FIND THE WAY HOME.

His desire to seek out those who are lost and who will turn to Him to find the way home. Even now, in the darkest time of history, Jesus is still seeking and saving all the lost who will turn to Him. If you feel lost, call out to Him. He will show you the way.

THE PRESENCE OF BIBLES AND BIBLICAL MATERIALS

There is another means—a silent witness—by which those who are left behind are hearing the good news of God's grace and forgiveness.

Millions upon millions of copies of the Bible and Bible portions have been published in all major languages, and distributed throughout the world. . . . Removal of believers from the world at the Rapture will not remove the Scriptures, and multitudes will no doubt be constrained to read the Bible. . . . Thus, multitudes will turn to their Creator and Savior in those days, and will be willing to give their testimony for the Word of God and even . . . their lives as they seek to persuade the world that the calamities it is suffering are judgments from the Lord. [4]

What all this shows is that God, in His mercy, is making sure that people everywhere on earth have an opportunity to hear the good news of the gospel of grace—through preachers, angels, and Christian materials and Bibles available all over the world. There is hope for you. I encourage you to avail yourself of these resources. Find a Bible and read it every day. Locate Christian books and materials that are consistent with the teachings of Scripture. Use whatever technology is available to access solid sermons and teachings about the end times.

Additionally, when you turn to Jesus, you can become another key link in the sharing of the good news of Jesus with others. Share this book with someone you know. You will certainly face strong opposition and deadly persecution, but don't let that deter you from extending the offer of eternal life to all who will listen to you. Your reward in heaven will be great.

WITNESS WITH A PROFOUND SENSE OF URGENCY. MAKE SURE YOU BRING AS MANY OTHER PEOPLE TO HEAVEN WITH YOU AS POSSIBLE. POINT THEM TO THE ONE WHO CAN SAVE.

I was thinking about you when I wrote this book. I knew from reading the Bible what you would face, and now it's coming to pass just as the Bible predicted. I'm in heaven now, and the pages you are reading are my legacy to you. I want you to find life and forgiveness in Jesus Christ. But not just for yourself and your family. I want you to come to Jesus and then go tell others who He is and what He has done for you. If you receive Jesus, you are now an ambassador of Jesus Christ. Reach out to those you know who are still without hope. Time is running out. Witness with a profound sense of urgency. Make sure you bring as many other people to heaven with you as possible. Your job is not to save others; you can't save anyone, but you can point them to the One who can save.

WHAT HAPPENS IF YOU DIE DURING THE TRIBULATION?

I hope you're convinced that you can be saved after the Rapture—that it's not too late for you to receive God's grace through Jesus Christ. Additionally, I know you see that following Jesus will exact a high price, even death. In light of these realities, you might be asking, "If I trust in Jesus as my Savior during the Tribulation and then die, what happens to me? Is there still hope after death?" The answer is that at the moment of death your soul immediately goes to heaven. Your body remains here on earth, but your soul rises immediately to heaven—to the presence of the Lord. The Bible says that to be absent from the body is to be present with the Lord (2 Corinthians 5:8).

The book of Revelation gives a glimpse into heaven where we see the souls of believers who are martyred during the Tribulation. They are waiting for God to exact vengeance on their persecutors who killed them.

> When He opened the fifth seal, I saw under the altar the souls of those who had been slain for the word of God and for the testimony which they held. And they cried with a loud voice, saying, "How long, O Lord, holy and true, until You judge and avenge our blood on those who dwell on the earth?" Then a white robe was given to each of them; and it was said to them that they should rest a little while longer, until both the number of their fellow servants and their brethren, who would be killed as they were, was completed. (Revelation 6:9–11)

The presence of martyred believers in heaven during the Tribulation is also presented in Revelation 7:15–16. "They are before the throne of God and serve him day and night in his temple; and he who sits on the throne will shelter them with his presence. 'Never again will they hunger; never again will they thirst. The sun will not beat down on them,' nor any scorching heat" (NIV). What an encouraging scene!

Seeing the incredible disasters the world is experiencing during the Tribulation, we can understand how these martyrs in heaven are praising the Lord with such fervor. Their troubles are over. They are home at last. This is in stark contrast to what happened to them on earth. They had been hungry, for they couldn't buy food without the mark of the Beast; they were thirsty, for the rivers were turned to blood; they were scorched by the burning sun. But now the agony of their lives is over. They are with the Lord.

When Jesus returns to earth at the end of the Tribulation the bodies of believers who die during the Tribulation will be resurrected and rejoined to their perfected spirit. Revelation 20:4 pictures these Tribulation believers in their new bodies. "And I saw thrones, and they sat on them, and judgment was committed to them. Then I saw the souls of those who had been beheaded for their witness to Jesus and for the word of God, who had not worshiped the beast or his image, and had not received his mark on their foreheads or on their hands. And they lived and reigned with Christ for a thousand years."

IS IT EVER TOO LATE TO BE SAVED?

One thing is crystal clear about salvation. If a person leaves this world without accepting Jesus Christ as Savior from sin, it's too late for that person to be saved. The soul of that person goes to hell forever. That's the plain yet painful truth. The Bible is clear. There is no second chance for salvation after death. As the old saying goes, "As death finds you, eternity keeps you." Nothing can change your fate after death. There is no purgatory and no parole.

Jesus clearly taught that death ends any opportunity to be saved. He told a story about a rich man, who failed to repent and turn to the Lord, and a poor man named Lazarus who knew the Lord. Both men died. The rich man went to hades, and Lazarus went to heaven to be with Abraham and all the saints. Jesus related a conversation in the afterlife between the rich man in hades and Abraham in heaven.

> "Then he cried and said, 'Father Abraham, have mercy on me, and send Lazarus that he may dip the tip of his finger in water and cool my tongue; for I am tormented in this flame.' But Abraham said, 'Son, remember that in your lifetime you received your good things, and likewise Lazarus evil things; but now he is comforted, and you are tormented. And besides all this, between us and you there is a great gulf fixed, so that those who want to pass from here to you cannot, nor can those from there pass to us.'" (Luke 16:24–26)

"A great gulf fixed"—a yawning chasm, an unbridgeable gulf, a gaping ravine. Those are arresting words. The boundaries of destiny are forever fixed in the afterlife. Death removes any opportunity to change your mind about your eternal destiny. Death closes the door of salvation forever.

But is there ever a time in this life when it's too late to be saved? Is there a line a person can cross that closes the window of salvation? I believe the answer to this solemn question is yes. The Bible contains a grave warning against all who reject Jesus Christ and receive the Antichrist during the Tribulation.

> And then the lawless one will be revealed, whom the Lord will consume with the breath of His mouth and destroy with the brightness of His coming. The coming of the lawless one is according to the working of Satan, with all power, signs, and lying wonders, and with all unrighteous deception among those who perish, because they did not receive the love of the truth, that they might be saved. And for this reason God will send them strong delusion, that they should believe the lie, that they all may be condemned who did not believe the truth but had pleasure in unrighteousness. (2 Thessalonians 2:8–12)

Those who embrace the lie of the Antichrist, that he is God, and are duped and deceived by his lying wonders, have no chance to be saved. It's over. Once the choice for Antichrist is made, God sends strong delusion to harden the choice and confirm the condemnation. There's no turning back from that fateful decision. It's irreversible and irrevocable. Their choice is set forever in the concrete of eternity.

Then a third angel followed them, saying with a loud voice, "If anyone worships the beast and his image, and receives his mark on his forehead or on his hand, he himself shall also drink of the wine of the wrath of God, which is poured out full strength into the cup of His indignation. He shall be tormented with fire and brimstone in the presence of the holy angels and in the presence of the Lamb. And the smoke of their torment ascends forever and ever; and they have no rest day or night, who worship the beast and his image, and whoever receives the mark of his name." (Revelation 14:9–11)

Whatever you do, don't listen to the siren song of the Antichrist, no matter how attractive it may seem. Resist him and receive Jesus. Encourage all those you know and love to do the same thing.

SERIOUS BUT NOT HOPELESS

On one occasion when he was prime minister, Winston Churchill had a brief meeting with his counterpart in the Republic of Ireland at a time when both countries were facing serious problems. When Churchill remarked to the Irish prime minister that, in his view, the situation in the United Kingdom was serious but not hopeless, the Irish prime minister replied that the situation in his country was hopeless but not serious.

When things get hopeless, they get serious. But thank God, while your situation is very serious, it's not hopeless. The bottom line of all we've said in this chapter is this: *As long as you resist the pull to accept the Antichrist as God, you can receive Christ, and He will graciously receive you if you come to Him.*

Hope is a person—Jesus Christ. It's been well said, "Life with Christ is an endless hope, without Him a hopeless end." As bad as things may look right now, you have an endless hope, a living hope, through the death and resurrection of Jesus. He is your only hope.

Dr. Arthur Compton was one of a committee of six scientists appointed by President Roosevelt to create the first atomic bomb. Later, in a magazine article, he recalled the day in 1942 when he and the other scientists conducted their first experiment in a squash court in Chicago. He described the different reactions—relief, concern, excitement—when the experiment was successful, and they realized that a power had been unleashed that would change the course of history. Compton knew that life on earth would never be the same. He concluded: "Man must now go the way of Jesus or perish."[5]

That's the choice for the world today, and it's your choice. Tragically, the world is perishing. But you can go the way of Jesus. Don't wait to receive Him. Time is passing. "Life is but a moment, a breath. It's the tick of a clock. A blink of an eye. A click of the fingers."[6] The Bible stresses the urgency to respond to the call of the gospel right now. "Behold, now is the accepted time; behold, now is the day of salvation" (2 Corinthians 6:2).

Paul Powell stresses the urgency: "Every page of the Bible says, 'today.' Every tick of the clock says, 'today.' Every beat of your heart says, 'today.' Every obituary column seems to cry out, 'today.' All of God's creation seems to cry out, 'Behold, today is the day of salvation.'"[7]

Is there any hope? *Yes!*

But only in Jesus.

YOUR PROMISE: Blessed be the God and Father of our Lord Jesus Christ, who according to His abundant mercy has begotten us again to a living hope through the resurrection of Jesus Christ from the dead, to an inheritance incorruptible and undefiled and that does not fade away, reserved in heaven for you. (1 Peter 1:3–4)

➤• MY PRAYER FOR YOU •➤

Father, You are abundant in lovingkindness and grace. Your mercies endure forever. They are new every morning, even in the darkest days. Even though Your children are tempted every day to give up hope and give in to despair, reassure their hearts by Your great power. If they are forced to give their lives for Jesus, give them a special measure of Your comfort, grace, and strength. Fill them with the hope of heaven. Give them opportunities and boldness to share the good news of Jesus with others who need Him. Amen.

In journalism the largest, boldest type ever used is called "second coming" type. The size and style jump off the page at the reader. It has been reserved for some of the major events of history, such as the Allied victory over the Nazis and the end of World War II. The reason it is called "second coming" type is simple. There is no event greater than the Second Coming of Jesus Christ back to earth, and apparently even the most irreligious journalists and liberal newspaper editors know it. Ironically, however, when Jesus comes, "Second Coming type will sit unused on the presses. Why? Because there will be no time to put out a flash street edition to announce His return."[1] Maybe social media will have time to briefly announce what's happening, but the world will probably be too awestruck to do anything but look up in stunned amazement.

7

WHAT ARE WE WAITING FOR?

ONE OF THE BEST STORIES I'VE HEARD ABOUT MEN LONGING FOR THEIR leader's return is that of explorer and adventurer Sir Ernest Shackleton. On Saturday, August 8, 1914, one week after Germany declared war on Russia, twenty-nine men set sail in a three-masted wooden ship from Plymouth, England, to Antarctica on a quest to become the first adventurers to cross the Antarctic continent on foot. Sir Ernest Shackleton had recruited the men through an advertisement: "Men Wanted for Hazardous Journey. Small wages. Bitter cold. Long months of complete darkness. Constant danger. Safe return doubtful. Honor and recognition in case of success."

Not only was Shackleton an honest man, for the men did experience all that his handbill promised, but he was also an able leader and a certified hero. His men came to refer to him as "the Boss," although he never thought of himself that way. He worked as hard as any crew member and built solid team unity aboard the ship, aptly named *Endurance*. In January 1915, the ship became entrapped in an ice pack and ultimately sank, leaving the men to set up camp on an ice floe—a flat, free-floating slice of sea ice.

Shackleton kept the men busy by day and entertained by night. They played ice soccer, had nightly songfests, and held regular sled-dog competitions. It was in the ice-floe camp that Shackleton proved his greatness as a leader. He willingly sacrificed his right to a warmer, fur-lined sleeping bag so that one of his men might have it, and he personally served hot milk to his men in their tents every morning.

In April 1916, their thinning ice floe threatened to break apart, forcing the men to seek refuge on nearby Elephant Island. Knowing that a rescue from such a desolate island was unlikely, Shackleton and five others left to cross eight hundred miles of open Antarctic sea in a twenty-foot lifeboat with more of a hope than a promise of a return with rescuers. Finally, on August 30, after an arduous 105-day trip and three earlier attempts, Shackleton returned to rescue his stranded crew, becoming their hero.

But perhaps the real hero in this story is Frank Wild. Second in command, Wild was left in charge of the camp in Shackleton's absence. He maintained the routine the Boss had established. He assigned daily duties, served meals, held sing-alongs, planned athletic competitions, and generally kept up morale. Because "the camp was in constant danger of being buried by the snow ... [and becoming] completely invisible from the sea, so that a rescue party might look for it in vain," Wild kept the men busy shoveling away drifts.

The firing of a gun was to be the prearranged signal that the rescue ship was near the island, but as Wild reported, "Many times when the glaciers were 'calving,' and chunks fell off with a report like a gun, we thought that it was the real thing, and after a time we got to distrust these signals." But he never lost hope in the return of the Boss. Confidently, Wild kept the last tin of kerosene and a supply of dry combustibles ready to ignite instantly for use as a locator signal when the "day of wonders" would arrive.

Barely four days' worth of rations remained in the camp when Shackleton finally arrived on a Chilean icebreaker. He personally made several trips through the icy waters in a small lifeboat in order to ferry his crew to safety. Miraculously, the leaden fog lifted long enough for all the men to make it to the icebreaker in one hour.

Shackleton later learned from the men how they were prepared to break camp so quickly and reported: "From a fortnight after I had left, Wild would roll up his sleeping bag each day with the remark, 'Get your things ready, boys, the Boss may come today.' And sure enough, one day the mist opened and revealed the ship for which they had been waiting and longing and hoping for over four months." Wild's "cheerful anticipation proved infectious," and all were prepared when the evacuation day came.[2]

Shackleton's stranded, beleaguered crew desperately hoped that their leader would come back to them, and they longed for his return. But as diligent and dedicated as Shackleton was, they could not be certain he would return. He was, after all, a mere man battling elements he could not control, so they knew he might not make it back.

Like that crew, you, too, are in a desperate condition. Time is running out. The Tribulation continues to get worse and worse. Yet, unlike that desperate crew, you have a certain promise that Jesus will return. Yours is not a mere longing or a desperate hope, as theirs was, because our Lord is the Creator and Master of all, and His promise is as sure as His very existence.

The return of Jesus is what you are waiting for, and it will be the greatest moment in history. Nothing else is even close. No words can adequately capture the splendor and brilliance of that moment when Jesus physically descends from heaven to earth. The joy of Shackleton's crew at the arrival of their leader will pale in comparison. All your hopes will be realized. That's what you are waiting for.

As you wait, the seven-year Tribulation period has unleashed a cascade and climax of worsening conditions, the anger of God against the wicked, and the signs of Christ's coming in judgment. The Antichrist is ruling wickedly. But just when it seems there is no hope, when the bottom is finally reached and evil rules, the Second Coming will finally come about, and God's Son will dethrone the Antichrist.

The Second Coming of Christ is a central theme of much of the Bible, and it is one of the best-attested promises in all of Scripture. You can rest in the sure conviction that just as Jesus came to earth the first time, and just as He came to rapture His followers to heaven before the Tribulation, so He will return at the conclusion of the Great Tribulation.

THE ANTICIPATION OF CHRIST

Although most people who know anything about Jesus or the Bible are most familiar with the first coming of Christ, that we celebrate at Christmas, Christ's second coming is mentioned more frequently in the Bible. References to the Second Coming outnumber references to the first by a factor of eight to one.

Scholars count 1,845 biblical references to the Second Coming, including 318 in the New Testament. Christ's return is emphasized in no less than seventeen Old Testament books and seven out of every ten chapters in the New Testament. The Lord Himself referred to His return twenty-one times. The Second Coming is second only to faith as the most dominant subject in the New Testament.

THE PROPHETS FORETOLD THE SECOND COMING OF CHRIST

While many of the Old Testament prophets wrote concerning the Second Coming of Christ, it is Zechariah who gave us the clearest and most concise prediction of it:

> Then the LORD will go forth
> And fight against those nations,
> As He fights in the day of battle.
> And in that day His feet will stand on the Mount
>   of Olives,
> Which faces Jerusalem on the east.
> And the Mount of Olives shall be split in two,
> From east to west,
> Making a very large valley;
> Half of the mountain shall move toward the north
> And half of it toward the south.
>   (Zechariah 14:3–4)

Notice how Zechariah deals in specifics, even pinpointing the geographic location where Christ will return: "In that day His feet will stand on the Mount of Olives" (14:4). Like Armageddon, the Mount of Olives is an explicitly identifiable place, just east of Jerusalem, that retains its ancient name even today. The prophet's specificity gives us confidence that his prophecy is true and accurate. But while Jesus will return to the Mount of Olives, the Bible is clear that every person on earth will see Him descend to earth (Revelation 1:7).

JESUS HIMSELF ANNOUNCED HIS SECOND COMING

Jesus, speaking from the Mount of Olives two days before He died on the cross, affirmed His Second Coming to His disciples in dramatic and cataclysmic terms:

"For as the lightning comes from the east and flashes to the west, so also will the coming of the Son of Man be. . . . Immediately after the tribulation of those days the sun will be darkened, and the moon will not give its light; the stars will fall from heaven, and the powers of the heavens will be shaken. Then the sign of the Son of Man will appear in heaven, and then all the tribes of the earth will mourn, and they will see the Son of Man coming on the clouds of heaven with power and great glory." (Matthew 24:27, 29–30)

In the fifteenth century the Turkish army overran Greece and took over Greek churches. Mosaics of Christ on the ceilings of the domes were plastered over. The mosaics were hidden for centuries. They were invisible from below yet still there all the time. Many were finally uncovered in the 1800s. Jesus was unveiled to onlookers for the first time in centuries.

Someday very soon, as promised, there will be an actual unveiling of Jesus Christ—an *apocalypse of Jesus Christ*—when He returns to earth in power and glory. Right now, He is hidden from below, but when the Tribulation has run its dreadful course, He will be revealed to the world just as He promised.

THE ANGELS ANNOUNCED THAT JESUS WOULD RETURN

Immediately following Christ's ascension into heaven at the end of His earthly ministry, two angels appeared to the stunned disciples and spoke words of comfort to them. "Men of Galilee," they said, "why do you stand gazing up into heaven? This same Jesus, who was taken up from you into heaven, will so come in like manner as you saw Him go into heaven" (Acts 1:11). The next verse tells us, "They returned to Jerusalem from the mount called Olivet" (v. 12). Did you catch that? Jesus ascended to heaven from the Mount of Olives (a small mountain just east of Jerusalem). According to the angels, Christ will return to that very same spot—the Mount of Olives. The words of the angels conveyed both comfort for the disciples' present loss of Jesus and confirmation of His future return.

JOHN THE APOSTLE FORETOLD JESUS' SECOND COMING

The prophecies of Christ's return are like bookends to the book of Revelation. In the first chapter John wrote: "Behold, He is coming with clouds, and every eye will see Him, even they who pierced Him. And all the tribes of the earth will mourn because of Him" (Revelation 1:7). And in the last pages of the last chapter—indeed, almost the last words of the New Testament—our Lord emphatically affirms His Second Coming: "He who testifies to these things says, 'Surely I am coming quickly.' Amen. Even so, come, Lord Jesus!" (22:20).

Obviously, you have every reason to anticipate the return of Christ. The Bible affirms it throughout as a certainty, describing it in specific terms and with ample corroboration.

THE ADVENT OF CHRIST

Let's look briefly at the Bible's description of the glory and majesty Christ will display at His second coming.

HIS DESIGNATION

In Revelation 19 the descending Lord is given three meaningful titles.

> Now I saw heaven opened, and behold, a white horse. And
> He who sat on him was called Faithful and True, and in

righteousness He judges and makes war. . . . He had a name written that no one knew except Himself. . . . and His name is called The Word of God. . . .And He has on His robe and on His thigh a name written: KING OF KINGS AND LORD OF LORDS. (vv. 11–13, 16)

I like the way one scholar summarizes these verses: "In these three names we have set forth first, our Lord's dignity as the Eternal Son; second, His incarnation—the Word became Flesh; and last, His second advent to reign as King of kings and Lord of lords."[3]

HIS DESCRIPTION

The eyes of the returning Christ are described as burning like a flame of fire, signifying His ability as a judge to see deeply into the hearts of men and ferret out all injustice (Revelation 1:14; 2:18; 19:12). His eyes will pierce through the motives of nations and individuals and judge them for what they really are—not for how they hope their masks of hypocrisy will make them appear!

Always remember that nothing is hidden from the eyes of Jesus. Everything and everyone are naked and open to His piercing gaze. Jesus sees us; Jesus sees through us. That means your sin is seen by Him, all of it. You cannot hide it. So when you sin you need to confess it to Him. The Bible says, "If we confess our sins, He is faithful and just to forgive us our sins and to cleanse us from all unrighteousness" (1 John 1:9). The word *confess* simply means "to say the same thing." When you confess your sin you are agreeing with God and saying the same thing about your sin that He says about it.

But not only does Jesus see your sin, He also sees your service for Him, and He will lavishly reward you for it someday in heaven.

> **JESUS SEES YOUR SERVICE FOR HIM, AND HE WILL LAVISHLY REWARD YOU FOR IT SOMEDAY IN HEAVEN.**

The head of the returning Christ is crowned with many crowns (Revelation 19:12), testifying to His status as the absolute sovereign King of kings and Lord of lords—the undisputed monarch of the entire earth.

He also wears a robe, which is dipped in blood, reminding us that He is the sacrificial Lamb of God. Earlier in Revelation, John described Him as "the Lamb slain from the foundation of the world" (13:8). In fact, Jesus will be represented to us as the Lamb of God, who died for our sins, throughout eternity.

HIS DESCENT

The Lord Jesus, captain of the Lord's hosts, will not descend to earth alone, as the following verses make abundantly clear:

- "Thus the LORD my God will come, and all the saints with You." (Zechariah 14:5)

- "The coming of our Lord Jesus Christ with all His saints." (1 Thessalonians 3:13)
- "Behold, the Lord comes with ten thousands of His saints." (Jude v. 14)

When Jesus returns to this earth to put down the world's ultimate rebellion, the armies of heaven will accompany him. John described these armies as "clothed in fine linen, white and clean, [following] Him on white horses" (Revelation 19:14). Those who were raptured to heaven by Jesus before the Tribulation will be part of the returning army accompanying the King.

In addition Jesus will bring the souls of all who die during the Tribulation with Him. Their perfected souls will be rejoined to their resurrected, immortal bodies. All those who have died in the Lord will join with the Lord and participate in the battle to reclaim the world for the rule of Christ.

The saints are not the only ones who will comprise the army of the Lord. Both Matthew and Paul told us that the angels will also descend with Christ. "When the Son of Man comes in His glory, and all the holy angels with Him, then He will sit on the throne of His glory" (Matthew 25:31); "and to give you who are troubled rest with us when the Lord Jesus is revealed from heaven with His mighty angels" (2 Thessalonians 1:7). How many angels are available for conscription into this army? Hebrews 12:22 sums it up by talking about innumerable angels in "joyful assembly" (NIV). Angels as far as the eye can see and the mind can imagine.[4]

THE AUTHORITY OF CHRIST

When the Lord returns to earth at the end of the Tribulation, the men and nations who have defied Him will no more be able to stand against Him than a spiderweb could stand against an eagle. His victory will be assured, and His authority undisputed. Here is how John described the finality of His judgment and the firmness of His rule: "And He Himself will rule them with a rod of iron. He Himself treads the winepress of the fierceness and wrath of Almighty God. And He has on His robe and on His thigh a name written: KING OF KINGS AND LORD OF LORDS" (Revelation 19:15–16).

This grand title, King of kings and Lord of lords, identifies our Lord at His second coming. It speaks of His unassailable authority. At this name every king on earth will bow, and every lord will kneel.

THE AVENGING OF CHRIST

The book of Revelation is divided into three sections. At the beginning of the book we are introduced to the world *ruined by humanity*. As we move to the latter half of the Tribulation period, we witness the world *ruled by Satan*. But now as we come to Christ's return at the end of the Tribulation period, we see the world *reclaimed by Christ*.

Reclaiming the earth, however, is not merely a simple matter of Christ stepping in and planting His flag. Before the earth can be reclaimed, it must be cleansed. You wouldn't move back into a house infested with rats without first exterminating and cleaning it up. That is what Christ must do before He reclaims the earth. All rebellion must be rooted out. He must avenge the damage done to His perfect creation by wiping the rebels from the face of the earth. The last verses of Revelation 19 give us an account of this purging and cleansing, and each step in the process is a dramatic story within itself. Let's briefly examine these avenging acts that will cleanse and reclaim the earth.

THE FOES OF HEAVEN

"And I saw the beast, the kings of the earth, and their armies, gathered together to make war against Him who sat on the horse and against His army" (Revelation 19:19). Could there be anything more futile and foolish than creatures fighting against their Creator? Than little men stuck on one tiny planet, floating in the immeasurable cosmos, striking back at the Creator of the universe? Yet futility is not beyond hearts turned away from God. John warned that the Antichrist and the False Prophet will persuade the armies of the earth to go to war against Christ and the armies of heaven. It's like persuading mice to declare war against lions. This final war will be the culmination of all of the rebellion that people have leveled against almighty God from the beginning of time! And there's not one iota of doubt about the outcome.

THE FATALITY OF THE BEAST AND THE FALSE PROPHET

The Bible tells us that God simply snatches up the Antichrist and the False Prophet and flings them into the fiery lake. "Then the beast was captured, and with him the false prophet who worked signs in his presence, by which he deceived those who received the mark of the beast and those who worshiped his image. These two were cast alive into the lake of fire burning with brimstone" (Revelation 19:20).

These two evil creatures have the unwanted honor of actually getting to hell before Satan, whose confinement occurs much later: "The devil, who deceived them, was cast into the lake of fire and brimstone where the beast and the false prophet are. And they will be tormented day and night forever and ever" (Revelation 20:10). Satan does not join the Beast and the False Prophet there until the end of the Millennium, one thousand years later.

Note that two men are taken alive. These two men are "cast into [the lake burning with fire and brimstone]" (20:10) where a thousand years later, they are still said to be "suffering the vengeance of eternal fire" (Jude 7). The lake of fire is neither annihilation nor purgatorial because it neither annihilates nor purifies these two fallen foes of God and man after a thousand years under judgment.[5]

THE FINALITY OF CHRIST'S VICTORY OVER REBELLION

"And the rest were killed with the sword which proceeded from the mouth of Him who sat on the horse" (Revelation 19:21). Here is how John F. Walvoord describes the victory:

When Christ returns at the end of the Tribulation period, the armies that have been fighting with each other for power will have invaded the city of Jerusalem and will have been engaged in house-to-house fighting. When the glory of the second coming of Christ appears in the heavens, however, these soldiers will forget their contest for power on earth and will turn to fight the army from heaven (16:16; 19:19). Yet their best efforts will be futile because Christ will smite them with the sword in His mouth (19:15, 21), and they will all be killed, along with their horses.[6]

THE APPLICATION OF CHRIST'S SECOND COMING

The prophets, the angels, and the apostle John all echoed the words of promise from Jesus Himself that He will return to earth at the end of the Tribulation. God's Word further amplifies the promise by giving you clues in prophecy to help you identify the signs that His return is close at hand—signs you are seeing right now all around you (Matthew 24:1–31).

Because of the high value I place on understanding Bible prophecy, I find that studying prophecy has an even higher and more practical value. It provides a compelling motivation for living for Christ, and even dying for Him, and looking for His coming. The immediacy of prophetic events shows the need to live each moment in Christlike readiness—even when the days grow dark and the nights long. Be encouraged! Be anticipating! You are secure; you belong to Christ if you have received Him as your Savior.

While there are many practical effects of the Second Coming for your life, here are three simple ones you can practice every day:

- **LET THE RETURN COMPEL YOU** to stand faithfully for Christ in the midst of oppression and persecution. Your King is coming.
- **LET THE RETURN COMFORT YOU** that evil will not prevail unchecked and that you have eternal hope.
- **LET THE RETURN CLEANSE YOU** to live a godly life in the midst of a corrupt culture.

Knowing Christ is coming again to this earth, you cannot go on being the same person. Think about this. If you survive the

Tribulation, you will be alive on earth when the victory train of Jesus slowly descends to earth. Every eye will see Him, including yours. No words can even come close to capturing what you will see, and hear, and feel. If you die during the Tribulation, you will return with Jesus as part of the victory train. Jesus will bring your perfected spirit with Him, resurrect your glorified body, and rejoin them into a brand-new existence. Either way, whether you die during the Tribulation or live until the Second Coming, you will be a part of this majestic event that will close out this age and usher in the kingdom of Jesus on earth.

Now that's something worth waiting for! Make sure you are ready.

Jesus came the first time to become your Savior, and He's coming the second time to be your King. The coming of Christ to set up His kingdom will be so much different than when He came before. Consider the contrast between His first and second comings. He entered the world the first time in swaddling clothes; He will reign the second time in majestic purple. He came the first time as a weary traveler; He will return the second time as the untiring God. Once when He came, He had nowhere to lay His head; when He comes back, He will be revealed as the heir of all things. Once He was rejected by tiny Israel; when He returns, He will be accepted by every single nation. Once He was a lowly Savior, acquainted with grief; then He will be the mighty God, anointed with the oil of gladness. Once He was smitten with a reed; then He will rule the nations with a rod of iron. Once wicked soldiers bowed the knee in mockery; then every knee will bow and every tongue confess that He is Lord. Once He received a crown of thorns; then He will receive a crown of gold. Once He delivered up His Spirit in death; then He will be alive forevermore. Once He was laid in a tomb; then He will sit on a throne. When He comes again, there will be no doubt and no delay. He will be "KING OF KINGS AND LORD OF LORDS" (Revelation 19:16).

> JESUS IS COMING THE SECOND TIME TO BE YOUR KING. PREPARE YOUR HEART NOW BY INSTALLING HIM AS KING OF YOUR LIFE.

You need to prepare your heart now by installing Him as King of your life. The Bible says one day "that at the name of Jesus every knee should bow, of those in heaven, and of those on earth, and of those under the earth, and that every tongue should confess that Jesus Christ is Lord, to the glory of God the Father" (Philippians 2:10–11).

YOUR PROMISE: "And behold, I am coming quickly, and My reward is with Me, to give to every one according to his work. I am the Alpha and the Omega, the Beginning and the End, the First and the Last." (Revelation 22:12–13)

➤• MY PRAYER FOR YOU •➤

Father, knowing without any doubt that Jesus is coming back fills Your children with hope and joy. Thank You. Thank You. Help them learn how to offer You their deepest praise and gratitude. Without the promise of the Second Coming, they would have no hope at all. Their lives would be shattered and meaningless. The horizon would hold nothing but the deepest despair. The return of Jesus changes everything for them. Keep them faithful to You even if it means giving their lives. Fill Your children with Your peace that passes all understanding as they watch, wait, and witness for Jesus. Even so, come Lord Jesus!

Most people don't realize that the Bible is a grand storybook. The Bible is the story of God. The biblical story, often called the metastory or the metanarrative, unfolds the story of God's reign over creation through humanity. The story opens with a happy beginning (Genesis 1–2). But a crisis occurs with the entrance of Satan and sin. God's solution to that crisis is the promise of a coming Redeemer who will deal with the sin problem and restore God's original plan for His creation (Genesis 3:15). The rest of the Bible is the rising plot of the coming Redeemer. The climax of the story is the arrival of the Redeemer, Jesus, on earth to die for sinful humanity and rise from the dead. In the end everything comes full circle when Jesus returns to earth to rule and reign over the world. The happy beginning is balanced by an equally happy ending. The Bible is a story with the ultimate happy ending—a happy ending for God's creation and a happy ending for you if you have put your trust in Jesus.

8

HOW WILL IT ALL END?

MARGUERITE HIGGINS WON THE PULITZER PRIZE FOR HER REPORTING AS a war correspondent during the Korean War. She wrote an account of the Fifth Company of Marines, with eighteen thousand men, who fought against more than a hundred thousand Chinese communists in savagely cold weather. She wrote:

It was particularly cold—42 degrees below zero—that morning when reporters were standing around. The weary soldiers, half frozen stood by their dirty trucks eating from tin cans. A huge marine was eating cold beans with his trench knife. His clothes were as stiff as a board. His face, covered with heavy beard, was crusted with mud. A correspondent asked him, "If I were God and could grant you anything you wished, what would you most like?" The man stood motion-less for a moment. Then he raised his head and replied, "Give me tomorrow."[1]

As the Tribulation rages, you may be feeling like that weary soldier. You're living—or maybe just surviving—day to day. You just want tomorrow—actually, a better tomorrow. You long for a better tomorrow. The good news I have for you, after a bunch of really bad news, is that when Jesus comes back to earth there will be a better tomorrow—the best tomorrow—for all of God's people.

While we can never fully envision, or wrap our minds around, the eternal future God has in store for His children, the time after the Second Coming of Jesus unfolds in sequence under three main banners, or captions, that will bring the best tomorrow possible.

- The Millennium
- The New Heaven and New Earth
- The New Jerusalem

These words probably don't mean much to you, but I pray that by the time we finish describing them they will fill you with comfort, excitement, and hope. Let me briefly sketch the outline of each of these future realities. I pray they will give you an eternal perspective to motivate and strengthen you to endure whatever you might face in the days ahead.

THE MILLENNIUM

The reclamation of planet earth begins with the golden age of Christ's reign. We often refer to this period of time by a certain title—the Millennium. Let's begin by taking the mystery out of the term *millennium*. The word *millennium* doesn't actually occur in most of our English Bibles. It comes to us from a combination of the Latin words *mille*, which means "a thousand," and *annum*, which means "years." The word *millennium*, then, simply means "a thousand years." The Millennium is a literal period of a thousand years, which is scheduled for the future and will begin when Jesus comes again at the end of history to set up His earthly kingdom.

During those ten centuries of righteousness, Christ will rule on earth from His capital in Jerusalem. To add to the excitement, John told us that the followers of Christ will receive rewards and will reign with Him. Our places of responsibility in that kingdom will be based on how we lived on earth. Scores of biblical promises reassure God's people they will receive rewards for faithful service. For instance, Isaiah 40:10 says, "Behold, the Lord GOD shall come with a strong hand, and His arm shall rule for Him; behold, His reward is with Him, and His work before Him." Jesus said, "The Son of Man will come in the glory of His Father with His angels, and then He will reward each according to his works" (Matthew 16:27). And Revelation 22:12 says, "I am coming quickly, and My reward is with Me, to give to every one according to his work."

The Bible teaches that when we serve the Lord here on earth as Christians we will be rewarded when we get to the kingdom with the opportunity to serve in a new and special way. Jesus taught that our role as servants and rulers will be based upon our faithfulness. Scripture tells us the words we want to hear from the Lord when we get to heaven: "Well done, good and faithful servant; you have been faithful over a few things, I will make you ruler over many things. Enter into the joy of your lord" (Matthew 25:23). These words will be part of our millennial experience. In the Millennium we will be ruling the earth with Jesus. He will be our King and we will serve Him, not as a punishment but as a reward. Randy Alcorn said:

> Service is a reward, not a punishment. This idea is foreign to people who dislike their work and only put up with it until retirement. We think that faithful work should be rewarded by a vacation for the rest of our lives. But God offers us something very different: more work, more responsibilities, increased

opportunities, along with greater abilities, resources, wisdom, and empowerment. We will have sharp minds, strong bodies, clear purpose, and unabated joy.[2]

Imagine the wonder of helping Jesus rule and reign on earth for a thousand golden years! Live today in light of that day.

FOUR PROFILES OF THE MILLENNIUM

What will the Millennium be like? How will we enjoy it? Imagine what it would be like on this earth if all sin were removed, if all rebellion were removed, if all unrighteousness were removed. These are the sorts of blessings the Millennium will bring, and the resulting conditions will be characterized by peace, prosperity, purity, and personal joy.

IT WILL BE A TIME OF PEACE

First, the Millennium will be a time of great peace. The Bible repeatedly speaks of the reign of peace.

- "In His days the righteous shall flourish, and abundance of peace." (Psalm 72:7)
- "For out of Zion the law shall go forth, and the word of the LORD from Jerusalem. He shall judge between many

peoples, and rebuke strong nations afar off; they shall beat their swords into plowshares, and their spears into pruning hooks; nation shall not lift up sword against nation, neither shall they learn war anymore." (Micah 4:2–3)

War will be utterly unknown during the earthly reign of Christ. Not a single armament plant will be operating. Not a soldier or sailor will be in uniform. No military camps will exist; not one cent will be spent on a military budget.

Christ's kingdom will be successful. There will be no revolutions, no political campaigns or party systems, and no decay. He will be a monarch without a successor, and it will be a kingdom without end. No dictator, uprising, or political coup d'état will oust this ruler. His kingdom will stand for a thousand years.

Is that really possible? Not here, not now—but when Jesus comes.

IT WILL BE A TIME OF PROSPERITY

The Millennium will also be a time of prosperity. The whole world will be economically healthy, and the land of Israel will flourish beyond anything imaginable. Once again, listen to the Word of God:

- "I will call for the grain and multiply it, and bring no famine upon you. And I will multiply the fruit of your trees and the increase of your fields, so that you need never again bear the reproach of famine among the nations." (Ezekiel 36:29–30)

- "'Behold, the days are coming,' says the LORD, 'when the plowman shall overtake the reaper, and the treader of grapes him who sows seed; the mountains shall drip with sweet wine, and all the hills shall flow with it.'" (Amos 9:13)

IT WILL BE A TIME OF PURITY

The Millennium will also be a wonderful time of holiness and purity. Sin will be kept in check and disobedience will be dealt with. Let me share some verses about that.

- "They shall not hurt nor destroy in all My holy mountain, for the earth shall be full of the knowledge of the LORD as the waters cover the sea." (Isaiah 11:9)
- "It shall come to pass that from one New Moon to another, and from one Sabbath to another, all flesh shall come to worship before Me." (Isaiah 66:23)
- "'It shall be in that day,' says the LORD of hosts, 'that I will cut off the names of the idols from the land, and they shall no longer be remembered. I will also cause the prophets and the unclean spirit to depart from the land.'" (Zechariah 13:2)

IT WILL BE A TIME OF PERSONAL JOY

Finally, the Millennium will be a time of personal joy, an exhilarating era of happiness and contentment. It will be the answer to many anguished prayers and many of the hopes you harbor in your heart today. Once again, let me offer Scripture to show you the preponderance of these truths in the Old Testament.

- "You have multiplied the nation and increased its joy; they rejoice before You according to the joy of harvest, as men rejoice when they divide the spoil." (Isaiah 9:3)
- "Therefore with joy you will draw water from the wells of salvation." (Isaiah 12:3)
- "The whole earth is at rest and quiet; they break forth into singing." (Isaiah 14:7)

During this thousand years, King Jesus will reign and rule on the throne of His ancestor David, in the city of Jerusalem. And out of Jerusalem will flow this wonderful reign of joy over all the world as we know it today. Can you imagine? Isn't it exhilarating to see what God has planned?

But here is the main thing: all this is simply the prelude to heaven. This is the front porch of eternity. It is a limited, advanced snapshot of what heaven will be like. The millennial earth will simply be a precursor or preview of the new earth.

When the Millennium ends, God will create a new heaven and new earth—a new universe.

THE NEW HEAVEN AND NEW EARTH

Utopia.

That strange word was coined more than five hundred years ago by Thomas More, a Roman Catholic philosopher, as the title of his fictional book describing a perfect society that existed on a remote island somewhere in the uncharted Atlantic. More invented the word *utopia* by combining the Greek term *ou*, meaning "no," with *topos*, meaning "place" (as in topological).

In other words Utopia is "no place," a nonexistent society that lives only in our dreams. Thomas More didn't picture Utopia as a perfect place, and scholars haven't been able to determine why he actually wrote the book or what it meant. Still, it's one of the most famous books in Western literature merely because of the word Thomas More coined for its title—*Utopia.*

After the publication of his book, that word entered the English lexicon to depict the concept of an idyllic place where things are somehow more perfect than we see them in our current world. People long for a more perfect world. We hear it in the dreams of the poets. We read it in literature. We see it in the paintings of the famous artists whose works fill the walls of the great museums of the world. It's as if we instinctively understand that our paradise in the garden of Eden was the normal state of affairs for humanity, but we lost it after Adam and Eve sinned against God. Now we yearn for its restoration. We want it back. We intuitively know things should be different than they are. We were made for a more perfect world. Jesus taught us to pray, "Your kingdom come. Your will be done on earth as it is in heaven" (Matthew 6:10).

Right now, during the Tribulation, the opposite is happening, but this prayer represents the hope in every heart. Whether we know it or not, we're homesick for the garden of Eden. In every beating heart there is a desire for what our first parents enjoyed—a perfect heaven on earth. We want everything restored that was lost. We can't help ourselves. It's programmed into the software of our humanity.

This often unspoken yearning corresponds with God's plans for the future, for everywhere we turn in the Bible we uncover prophecies and predictions about God's true utopia—the new heaven and the new earth, wherein righteousness dwells.

THE PROMISE OF THE NEW HEAVEN AND THE NEW EARTH

The apostle Peter excitedly described the dramatic events leading up to the new heaven and the new earth:

The heavens and the earth which are now preserved by the same word, are reserved for fire until the day of judgment and perdition of ungodly men. . . . But the day of the Lord will come as a thief in the night, in which the heavens will pass away with a great noise, and the elements will melt with fervent heat; both the earth and the works that are in it will be burned up. Therefore, since all these things will be dissolved, what manner of persons ought you to be in holy conduct and godliness, looking for and hastening the coming of the day of God, because of which the heavens will be dissolved, being on fire, and the elements will melt with fervent heat? Nevertheless we, according to His promise, look for new heavens and a new earth in which righteousness dwells. (2 Peter 3:7, 10–13)

Out of this purged mass of God's creative work, He will reshape, He will remake, He will re-create all of the heavens and this earth. There will be no destruction of what God has made. It is a renewal. It is a renaissance. It is a regeneration. It is a re-creation.

God will draw the curtains on human history, and the entire universe will undergo a purifying conflagration. All evidence of disease will be burned up. All evidence of disobedience will melt away. All the remnants and results of sin, sorrow, and suffering will be destroyed. Out of the smoldering ruins, God will re-create all physical reality, and He will bring forth a fresh universe—a new heaven and a new earth.

REALIZING THAT EVERYTHING AROUND YOU IS TEMPORARY SHOULD SHIFT YOUR FOCUS, REALIGN YOUR VALUES, AND PURIFY YOUR LIFE.

Visualize this passage. Think in terms of an apocalyptic movie in which the world and, indeed, the whole universe explodes and collapses into flames, and somehow out of the cataclysm a new heaven and a new earth appear.

This prepares us for the Bible's greatest passage on the new heaven and new earth: Revelation 21–22. Look at the way John began this final section of Scripture: "Now I saw a new heaven and a new earth, for the first heaven and the first earth had passed away. Also there was no more sea. Then I, John, saw the holy city, New Jerusalem, coming down out of heaven from God, prepared as a bride adorned for her husband" (21:1–2).

We can't fully conceive of what this will be like, and we struggle to imagine what it will look like. But use your God-given imagination and take these God-given words into your heart. Picture them. See the current ages drawing to a close, the universe collapsing like an old house in flames, a new earth emerging from the carnage, and a new city glistening and descending and ready to lead us into eternity with Jesus on the throne. Talk about utopia! That word is hopelessly insufficient to describe the place God is preparing for us. It is our heavenly home—the place where Christ rules forever.

THE PRINCIPLES OF THE NEW HEAVEN AND NEW EARTH

When this new creation is finished and God has purified it, it's still the same earth and still the same heaven, but it will have been purged. It will be made fresh. All the stains of sin will be gone. All the evidences of death. All the signs of disease. What, then, will the world be like? Among the glorious things we're told in the book of Revelation, two have struck me with particular force—the reversal of the curse and the restoration of all things.

THE REVERSAL OF THE CURSE

We uncover another glorious feature of the new world with these words in Revelation 22:3: "And there shall be no more curse, but the throne of God and of the Lamb shall be in it, and His servants shall serve Him." When John used the word *curse* he was pointing back to the words God spoke in the garden of Eden in Genesis 3, after Adam and Eve had rebelled and brought sin and shame upon the world.

The curse is why everything goes wrong in our world and why life is such a fight all the time. Humanity always has to run uphill, and nature often works against us. In a million ways we see the earth deteriorating around us. Look at an empty field. It doesn't sprout into flowerbeds or ornamental gardens; it descends into a patch of weeds. Look at our human bodies. At a certain point, they begin to deteriorate, age, break down, and fail. Look across our planet at the ravages of droughts, earthquakes, hurricanes, tornadoes, fires, and floods—not to mention the evils perpetuated by humanity's sinful nature. All this is summed up in that one word: *curse*.

Now think of the power of these words from Revelation 22:3: "And there shall be no more curse." When we get to the new heaven and the new earth, the curse will be reversed. It will be lifted; it will be dispelled forever. Oh, think of it! The weariness that accompanies our work will be a forgotten memory. Nature will work as it should, the weather will always be in our favor, and the ground will grow flowers as naturally as it produces thorns and thistles today. We ourselves will not fall into the ground in death because we will never die. God sent His Son into the world, not only to save our souls but also to redeem creation from the results of sin. The work of Christ goes beyond the incredible goal of saving an innumerable throng of blood-bought people.

The total work of Christ is nothing less than redeeming this entire creation from the effects of sin. That purpose will not be accomplished until God has ushered in the new earth, until paradise lost becomes paradise regained. But it will be accomplished!

We can live with these things now because there's a day when we will live without them.

THE RESTORATION OF ALL THINGS

That brings us to the second feature I want to mention about the new heaven and the new earth—the restoration of all things. Revelation 21:4–5 says, "The former things have passed away. Then He who sat on the throne said, 'Behold, I make all things new.'"

Randy Alcorn explained it like this:

Heaven is God's home. Earth is our home. Jesus Christ, as the God-man, forever links God and mankind, and thereby forever links Heaven and Earth. As Ephesians 1:10 demonstrates, this idea of Earth and Heaven becoming one is explicitly biblical. Christ will make Earth into Heaven and Heaven into Earth. Just as the wall that separates God and mankind is torn down in Jesus, so too the wall that separates Heaven and Earth will be forever demolished. There will be one universe, with all things in Heaven and on Earth together under one head, Jesus Christ.

Alcorn continued, "God's plan is that there will be no more gulf between the spiritual and physical worlds. There will be no divided loyalties or divided realms. There will be one cosmos, one universe united under one Lord—forever. This is the unstoppable plan of God. This is where history is headed."[3]

In his narrative about heaven, David Haney wrote about going to his favorite restaurant in Dallas, Texas, that features creative Southwestern cuisine. The most famous item on the menu is a specially prepared rib eye steak, but the restaurant is also known for its extensive menu of exotic appetizers. One day David sat down at his table, studied the menu, and ordered a marvelous shrimp fajita appetizer that was unlike anything he had ever tasted in his life. "I discovered taste buds that I did not even know I had," he said. "I could not believe that anyone could make something so odd-sounding taste so good."

When the waiter returned to inquire about the entrée, David told him he didn't want to eat anything else all night. The shrimp fajita had done him in, and he didn't even plan to brush his teeth that evening because he wanted to savor the memory of the marvelous taste. But the waiter told him, "If you thought that was good, just wait for the rib eye."[4]

Afterward David thought about that simple conversation, and he pondered the whole idea of "foretaste." In a sense, the beauties of our world—the hills, the plains, the mountains, the oceans, the spangling vault of heaven—are like appetizers that whet our appetites for the main course, for God's new creation. I don't know anything more about these realities than what the Bible tells us; Scripture is our only source of truth about the life hereafter. But based upon these biblical truths, I believe the same God who magnificently created this present world is preparing for that moment when He will make all things new. The scene in Revelation 21 and 22 is not some fictional utopia. It is absolute reality, revealed for us in God's book, designed for us by God's heart, and provided for us by God's own Son.

I'm doing my best to present what the Bible tells you about the eternal future for God's people, but I'm sure you can see that human words are completely insufficient and inadequate. God has graciously given us enough information to whet our spiritual appetites about

GOD HAS GRACIOUSLY GIVEN US ENOUGH INFORMATION TO WHET OUR SPIRITUAL APPETITES ABOUT LIFE IN ETERNITY.

life in eternity. Nevertheless, even God has told us that in this life we cannot grasp the glory of what He has prepared for us. "Eye has not seen, nor ear heard, nor have entered into the heart of man the things which God has prepared for those who love Him" (1 Corinthians 2:9). I can only imagine!

THE NEW JERUSALEM

The apostle John not only told us of the creation of the new heaven and the new earth, but also that the great city of New Jerusalem will descend from the sky and become the capital city of God's eternal kingdom. It's important to realize that the city of New Jerusalem is not really heaven, per se. It is the capital city of heaven. The Bible delights in telling us about this place, which is also called the celestial city or Mount Zion. The final two chapters of the Bible use the word *city* eleven times to describe our eternal home, and I don't believe it's a figure of speech. It is an actual physical place—a real city. Since our resurrected bodies will be physical bodies, real and tangible, they will need a real place and an actual home—a physical city. History began in a garden and ends in a city.

Here, in one of the Bible's most climactic passages, this great city is described as it descends, fully designed and built, to the earth:

> Now I saw a new heaven and a new earth, for the first heaven and the first earth had passed away. Also there was no more sea. Then I, John, saw the holy city, New Jerusalem, coming down out of heaven from God, prepared as a bride adorned for her husband. And I heard a loud voice from heaven saying, "Behold, the tabernacle of God is with men, and He will

dwell with them, and they shall be His people. God Himself will be with them and be their God. And God will wipe away every tear from their eyes; there shall be no more death, nor sorrow, nor crying. There shall be no more pain, for the former things have passed away." Then He who sat on the throne said, "Behold, I make all things new." And He said to me, "Write, for these words are true and faithful." (Revelation 21:1–5)

This description implies that the holy city was designed, built, and ready-made for the new earth. John did not see the New Jerusalem created; he said he saw the city already built and coming down out of the highest heaven. In other words the New Jerusalem is an actual, physical city presently located within the third heaven. Jesus referred to New Jerusalem in Revelation 3:12 as the "city of My God." Here in Revelation 21, John saw this city descending to the new earth. This city of New Jerusalem is the place Jesus is preparing for us.

THE DIMENSIONS OF THE CITY

Sometimes people ask me, "How in the world can heaven be large enough to hold all the redeemed of all the ages?" Well, first of all, I assume the entirety of the new heaven and new earth will be inhabitable. But if we limit our thinking simply to the city of New Jerusalem, our minds are still boggled by its immensity. Revelation 21:15–16 says, "He who talked with me had a gold reed to measure the city, its gates, and its wall. The city is laid out as a square; its length is as great as its breadth. And he measured the city with the reed: twelve thousand furlongs. Its length, breadth, and height are equal."

In today's terms that means New Jerusalem will be about 1,500 miles wide, 1,500 miles long, and 1,500 miles high. That's more than 2 million square miles on the first "floor" alone! And given that this city is cubical and rises far beyond the stratosphere (the stratosphere starts about eleven miles above the surface of the earth; New Jerusalem ascends to 1,500 miles), we can assume that in some way it will have more than one level. There will be vertical elements to it. To me, one of the most amazing things about the dimensions of this city involves its height. According to Revelation 21:16, it is just as high as it is long and wide, which means it will ascend 1,500 miles into the air.

And that's just the capital city! Don't forget what's all around it—the new heaven and the new earth. Some people are over-whelmed as they begin to wonder how we'll ever get around in a city like that. We're used to the congestion and traffic jams of earth. But remember what we said about our new bodies. We may have the ability, like Christ, to travel instantly and by the impulses of thought. Transportation will be no problem. I don't want to become too speculative, but I want you to share my excitement about the sheer, overwhelming, mind-boggling size of the city. It will exceed anything we've ever imagined.

THE DESCRIPTION OF THE CITY

The dimensions of this vast city serve as only the beginning point of our observations. As we continue reading through Revelation 21 and 22, we're awestruck by the multifaceted descriptions of the city. I encourage you to read these final two chapters of Scripture for yourself and make them an object of ongoing study to give you strength for today and bright hope for tomorrow. To help you, I want to point out the sevenfold depiction these chapters give us of New Jerusalem. On that basis, then, let's look at these seven wonderful features of New Jerusalem.

THE HOLY CITY

First, this will be a holy city. Notice the emphasis on this in Revelation 21:

- "Then I, John, saw the holy city, New Jerusalem." (v. 2)
- "And he carried me away in the Spirit to a great and high mountain, and showed me the great city, the holy Jerusalem, descending out of heaven from God." (v. 10)

The chief characteristic of this city is its holiness. *The Wycliffe Bible Commentary* says, "A holy city will be one in which no lie will be uttered in one hundred million years, no evil word will ever be spoken, no shady business deal will ever even be discussed, no unclean picture will ever be seen, no corruption of life will ever be manifest. It will be holy because everyone in it will be holy."[5]

Without sin, there will be no death. There will be no jails, courtrooms, prisons, hospitals, or funeral homes in heaven. This is a holy place for holy people, for those who have been made holy by God's infinite grace through the blood of Jesus Christ.

THE GATES OF PEARL

The Bible also tells us about a vast, high, broad wall surrounding New Jerusalem, punctuated by twelve gates, each of which is made of pearl (Revelation 21:17–21). Perhaps you're wondering what kind of oyster is required to produce such a gigantic pearl! But do you think God is limited to creating pearls only by oysters? God can make a pearl just by speaking a word if He wishes. If He can speak a word and create a star, He can certainly do so with pearls. That said, I'm not sure how God will do it, but each of the twelve gates will be as beautiful and stunning as a giant pearl. Think of it. The wall is made of jasper, which, in biblical times, was a crystal stone like a diamond, and the gigantic gates are made of solid pearl. Imagine seeing this from afar. It will sparkle and shine as it rotates down to the earth, and all the hues of the glory of the city will be overwhelming. It will take your breath away.

When the famous Puritan John Owen was on his deathbed, his secretary wrote (in his name) to a friend, "I am still in the land of the living." But suddenly Owen said to his secretary, "Stop." Then he said, "Change that and say, I am yet in the land of the dying, but I hope soon to be in the land of the living."[6] I love that. We think we are in the land of the living going to the land of the dying. But really we are in the land of the dying, going to the land of the living. We call what we experience now "life" and the next stage as the "afterlife." But if you know Jesus, what you are experiencing now is "before life" and what awaits you is "life." You and I will only know all that life was intended to be after Jesus returns to earth to make all things new.

> YOU AND I WILL ONLY KNOW ALL THAT LIFE WAS INTENDED TO BE AFTER JESUS RETURNS TO EARTH TO MAKE ALL THINGS NEW.

THE FOUNDATIONS OF PRECIOUS STONES

The third descriptive element of this city is its foundation. Revelation 21:19–20 describes it this way: "The foundations of the wall of the city were adorned with all kinds of precious stones: the first foundation was jasper, the second sapphire, the third chalcedony, the fourth emerald, the fifth sardonyx, the sixth sardius, the seventh chrysolite, the eighth beryl, the ninth topaz, the tenth chrysoprase, the eleventh jacinth, and the twelfth amethyst."

They certainly describe a set of stones with all the colors and hues of the rainbow. Can you imagine approaching heaven's capital and seeing it from afar? It will shimmer and sparkle with the glory of God. We'll witness this magnificent city, soaring 1,500 miles into the atmosphere, built upon gemstone foundations, with each gate brilliantly crafted from a single pearl. We'll walk into this holy city with jaws dropped and eyes widened in absolute wonder, for even the most beautiful places on earth don't hold a candle to what God has prepared for us.

THE STREETS OF GOLD

But that's not all! Revelation 21 also says the city is constructed of gold, and even its central boulevard will be made of solid gold paving stones: "The twelve gates were twelve pearls: each individual gate was of one pearl. And the street of the city was pure gold, like transparent glass" (v. 21). Interestingly, the gold of New Jerusalem is described as being like "transparent glass." The earthly gold that currently fills our vaults isn't transparent, of course, but the gold of heaven will be so pure that we will seem to look into it and through its clear depths as we walk upon it. Some scholars interpret this as being like a finely polished mirror and therefore not so much transparent as translucent. But remember: we'll be walking around in our glorified bodies, and we can assume our eyesight will be enhanced so we can see things as we've never seen them before.

THE LAMB THAT IS THE LIGHT

The next thing we encounter in Revelation 21 and 22 has to do with the light and energy sources for the city of New Jerusalem. Where will its power plant be located? Where will its electrical generators be? How can such an immense city be illumined? Four different verses are devoted to this subject:

- "Her light was like a most precious stone, like a jasper stone, clear as crystal." (Revelation 21:11)
- "The city had no need of the sun or of the moon to shine in it, for the glory of God illuminated it. The Lamb is its light." (Revelation 21:23)
- "And the nations of those who are saved shall walk in its light." (Revelation 21:24)
- "There shall be no night there: They need no lamp nor light of the sun, for the Lord God gives them light." (Revelation 22:5)

There will be no light posts in New Jerusalem, no lanterns, no floodlights or flashlights or table lights. A strange presence of brilliant light will emanate throughout the city from the throne of God and of the Lamb. The brilliance of the light will beam forth from the Lord Jesus in His glorification, and it will fill the city with radiance. Were it not for our new glorified eyesight, we would be blinded. But it won't hurt our eyes at all; in fact, our new eyes will be perfectly made for such light. I can't imagine that, but I can anticipate it.

This is the New Jerusalem described in Scripture, and it's the fulfillment of a prophecy made hundreds of years before the birth of Christ, in Isaiah 60:19: "The sun shall no longer be your light by day, nor for brightness shall the moon give light to you; but the LORD will be to you an everlasting light, and your God your glory."

THE TREE OF LIFE

There's another wonderful feature of this city—the presence of the Tree of Life. Revelation 22:2 says, "In the middle of its street, and on either side of the river, was the tree of life, which bore twelve fruits, each tree yielding its fruit every month. The leaves of the tree were for the healing of the nations." One of the topographical features of New Jerusalem is a river flowing down from the throne of God, its waters as clear as crystal; and on both sides of the river are the trees of life—not just one tree but multiple trees.

Notice that verse two refers to "each tree." The Greek term

indicates a plurality of the trees, such as we'd find in an orchard. These trees will bear fruit every month, and it will be like eating fruit from the garden of Eden.

THE RIVER OF LIFE

That brings us to the final feature in our tour of New Jerusalem—the river of life. Look at Revelation 22:1: "He showed me a pure river of water of life, clear as crystal, proceeding from the throne of God and of the Lamb."

The new city of Jerusalem—the heavenly Zion—will have a river of waters that are clear as crystal, flowing from the throne of God. It will be the most beautiful river ever created in time or eternity. This is our destination, our eternal home.

Think of the most beautiful spot you've ever seen on earth. For me it's a place called Santorini. My wife, Donna, and I took a little break a few years ago and visited Greece and Turkey. One of the Greek islands in the southern Aegean Sea is Santorini, a volcanic island only about thirty-five square miles in size. As we stood on the deck of the boat and looked at the blindingly white little town with its rounded roofs and quaint simplicity, elevated along the clifftops above the blue sea and jutting upward toward the blue sky, it almost appeared to be suspended in space.

"Wow," we said, "what a beautiful place!" But it doesn't compare to what God has envisioned for those who have put their trust in Him.

THE DOOR TO THE CITY

You might be surprised to learn that heaven is not for everyone. The only people allowed in this city are those whose names are written in the Lamb's Book of Life. There are no exceptions. You won't be able to argue your way into that city, or con your way in, or sneak in, or bribe your way in. If you have not accepted God's plan for your life and received His forgiveness for your sin, when the moment comes, you will be denied entrance into heaven and into the city we have described. I don't want that to happen to you!

Heaven is real. Have you made your reservation? I urge you to do that now! The final invitation in the book of Revelation says:

> And the Spirit and the bride say, "Come!" And let him who hears say, "Come!" And let him who thirsts come. Whoever desires, let him take the water of life freely. (22:17)

Take the Water of Life now. Take Jesus. He will quench your spiritual thirst forever.

What you are facing now, and in the days ahead, is dark and depressing. Corrie ten Boom, who survived a Nazi concentration camp, once said, "The worst can happen, but the best remains." What a glorious reality. While the worst may be happening to you, remember, the best remains.

JESUS IS THE KEY

A father was sitting on the sofa watching a football game on television, when his little boy came running over. "Daddy, can you play with me?"

Though the dad enjoyed playing with his son, and planned to give him plenty of time, he was busy. The game was in the fourth quarter. "Soon, son, soon," said Dad. "When the game is over."

Five minutes later the little boy returned. "Daddy, can we play now?"

"Soon, son, soon. When the game is over."

Two minutes later the little boy returned again. "Daddy, is it time to play yet?"

The dad realized he was not going to get any peace, so he decided to give his son a task that would occupy his time. He noticed a picture of the world on the front page of the newspaper lying on the coffee table. He tore the picture out, then ripped it into small pieces. "Now, son, I've got a game for you. Take the pieces of this picture of the world and put them back together again and then we'll play together."

The little boy eagerly took the pieces away with him and got to work. Relieved, the dad turned back to his game. He would get to see the last few minutes. But to his amazement his little boy returned in less than five minutes. "I've finished, Daddy. Can we play now?"

The father was stunned as he turned around to see his son holding up the picture of the world, each piece sticky-taped into the right position. The dad began wondering whether he had a child prodigy on his hands. "How did you get it done so quickly?" he asked.

"Oh, it was easy, Daddy. On the back of the world was a picture of Jesus, so I put Jesus together and that's when the world came together."[7]

Right now, the world is falling apart. It's being ripped in pieces. And it can never come together or make sense apart from Jesus. When Jesus returns to earth, the world, which reeled under the weight of the Tribulation, will be put back together by Him, and it also means that *your* world will be put together by Him. That means regardless of what happens—no matter how depressing or difficult things might be right now—life in Christ has a happy ending for those who have received Him as Savior. For every believer the best is yet to come.

There *is* a better, eternal tomorrow in Jesus Christ.

Make sure you have personally come to Jesus for salvation from your sins and the free gift of eternal life. If you have not done so yet, you can receive Him right now and join God's family.

Admit that you are a sinner—that you need Him.

Acknowledge Jesus as your Savior—that you cannot save yourself.

Accept Jesus as your Savior by calling out to Him and receiving Him.

If you've done that, here is God's eternal promise to you. "But as many as received Him, to them He gave the right to become children of God, to those who believe in His name" (John 1:12).

YOUR PROMISE: "He who has an ear, let him hear what the Spirit says to the churches. To him who overcomes I will give to eat from the tree of life, which is in the midst of the Paradise of God." (Revelation 2:7)

◆• MY PRAYER FOR YOU •◆

Father, thank You for the hope of a better tomorrow through Jesus Christ. As the world around Your children falls apart, thank You that in Jesus someday the world will be put back together and that the world will be put back together far better than they can ever imagine. As they wait and anticipate Christ's coming to make all things new, give them Your eyes to look beyond what is seen to see the unseen—to see beyond the temporal to the eternal. Cover Your children with Your strength, insight, direction, and blessing as they wait for all things to be made new.

KEY SCRIPTURES TO HELP YOU THROUGH THESE TIMES

ANXIETY / WORRY

Cast your burden on the LORD, and He shall sustain you; He shall never permit the righteous to be moved.

PSALM 55:22

"Therefore I say to you, do not worry about your life, what you will eat or what you will drink; nor about your body, what you will put on. Is not life more than food and the body more than clothing? Look at the birds of the air, for they neither sow nor reap nor gather into barns; yet your heavenly Father feeds them. Are you not of more value than they? Which of you by worrying can add one cubit to his stature? So why do you worry about clothing? Consider the lilies of the field, how they grow: they neither toil nor spin; and yet I say to you that even Solomon in all his glory was not arrayed like one of these. Now if God so clothes the grass of the field, which today is, and tomorrow is thrown into the oven, will He not much more clothe you, O you of little faith? Therefore do not worry, saying, 'What shall we eat?' or 'What shall we drink?' or 'What shall we wear?' For after all these things the Gentiles seek. For your heavenly Father knows that you need all these things. But seek first the kingdom of God and His righteousness, and all these things shall be added to you. Therefore do not worry about tomorrow, for tomorrow will worry about its own things. Sufficient for the day is its own trouble."

MATTHEW 6:25–34

Be anxious for nothing, but in everything by prayer and supplication, with thanksgiving, let your requests be made known to God; and the peace of God, which surpasses all understanding, will guard your hearts and minds through Christ Jesus.

PHILIPPIANS 4:6–7

Casting all your care upon Him, for He cares for you.

1 PETER 5:7

DIRECTION / GUIDANCE

I will instruct you and teach you in the way you should go; I will guide you with My eye.

PSALM 32:8

The steps of a good man are ordered by the LORD, and He delights in his way. Though he fall, he shall not be utterly cast down; for the LORD upholds him with His hand.

PSALM 37:23–24

Your word is a lamp to my feet and a light to my path.

PSALM 119:105

Your ears shall hear a word behind you, saying, "This is the way, walk in it," whenever you turn to the right hand or whenever you turn to the left.

ISAIAH 30:21

If any of you lacks wisdom, let him ask of God, who gives to all liberally and without reproach, and it will be given to him.

JAMES 1:5

FEAR

"Have I not commanded you? Be strong and of good courage; do not be afraid, nor be dismayed, for the LORD your God is with you wherever you go."

JOSHUA 1:9

Yea, though I walk through the valley of the shadow of death, I will fear no evil; for You are with me; Your rod and Your staff, they comfort me.

PSALM 23:4

God is our refuge and strength, a very present help in trouble. Therefore we will not fear, even though the earth be removed, and though the mountains be carried into the midst of the sea.

PSALM 46:1–2

"Fear not, for I am with you; be not dismayed, for I am your God. I will strengthen you, yes, I will help you, I will uphold you with My righteous right hand."

ISAIAH 41:10

But now, thus says the LORD, who created you, O Jacob, and He who formed you, O Israel: "Fear not, for I have redeemed you; I have called you by your name; you are Mine. When you pass through the waters, I will be with you; and through the rivers, they shall not overflow you. When you walk through the fire, you shall not be burned, nor shall the flame scorch you."

ISAIAH 43:1–2

FORGIVENESS

Blessed is he whose transgression is forgiven, whose sin is covered. Blessed is the man to whom the LORD does not impute iniquity, and in whose spirit there is no deceit. When I kept silent, my bones grew old through my groaning all the day long. For day and night Your hand was heavy upon me; my vitality was turned into the drought of summer. *Selah*. I acknowledged my sin to You, and my iniquity I have not hidden. I said, "I will confess my transgressions to the LORD," and You forgave the iniquity of my sin. *Selah*.

PSALM 32:1–5

Bless the LORD, O my soul, and forget not all His benefits: Who forgives all your iniquities.

PSALM 103:2–3

He will again have compassion on us, and will subdue our iniquities. You will cast all our sins into the depths of the sea.

MICAH 7:19

And be kind to one another, tenderhearted, forgiving one another, even as God in Christ forgave you.

EPHESIANS 4:32

"Their sins and their lawless deeds I will remember no more."

HEBREWS 10:17

GOD'S LOVE

Because Your lovingkindness is better than life, my lips shall praise You.

PSALM 63:3

"For God so loved the world that He gave His only begotten Son, that whoever believes in Him should not perish but have everlasting life."

JOHN 3:16

But God demonstrates His own love toward us, in that while we were still sinners, Christ died for us.

ROMANS 5:8

Yet in all these things we are more than conquerors through Him who loved us. For I am persuaded that neither death nor life, nor angels nor principalities nor powers, nor things present nor things to come, nor height nor depth, nor any other created thing, shall be able to separate us from the love of God which is in Christ Jesus our Lord.

ROMANS 8:37–39

God is love.

1 JOHN 4:8

HEAVEN

"Let not your heart be troubled; you believe in God, believe also in Me. In My Father's house are many mansions; if it were not so, I would have told you. I go to prepare a place for you. And if I go and prepare a place for you, I will come again and receive you to Myself; that where I am, there you may be also."

JOHN 14:1–3

But as it is written: "Eye has not seen, nor ear heard, nor have entered into the heart of man the things which God has prepared for those who love Him."

1 CORINTHIANS 2:9

For here we have no continuing city, but we seek the one to come.

HEBREWS 13:14

Immediately I was in the Spirit; and behold, a throne set in heaven, and One sat on the throne.

REVELATION 4:2

And he showed me a pure river of water of life, clear as crystal, proceeding from the throne of God and of the Lamb. In the middle of its street, and on either side of the river, was the tree of life, which bore twelve fruits, each tree yielding its fruit every month. The leaves of the tree were for the healing of the nations. And there shall be no more curse, but the throne of God and of the Lamb shall be in it, and His servants shall serve Him. They shall see His face, and His name shall be on their foreheads. There shall be no night there: They need no lamp nor light of the sun, for the Lord God gives them light. And they shall reign forever and ever.

REVELATION 22:1–5

HOPE

Why are you cast down, O my soul? And why are you disquieted within me? Hope in God; for I shall yet praise Him, the help of my countenance and my God.

PSALM 42:11

Now hope does not disappoint, because the love of God has been poured out in our hearts by the Holy Spirit who was given to us.

ROMANS 5:5

Now may the God of hope fill you with all joy and peace in believing, that you may abound in hope by the power of the Holy Spirit.

ROMANS 15:13

Let us hold fast the confession of our hope without wavering, for He who promised is faithful.

HEBREWS 10:23

Blessed be the God and Father of our Lord Jesus Christ, who according to His abundant mercy has begotten us again to a living hope through the resurrection of Jesus Christ from the dead.

1 PETER 1:3

PEACE

The peace of God, which surpasses all understanding, will guard your hearts and minds through Christ Jesus.

PHILIPPIANS 4:7

I will both lie down in peace, and sleep; for You alone, O LORD, make me dwell in safety.

PSALM 4:8

You will keep him in perfect peace, whose mind is stayed on You, because he trusts in You.

ISAIAH 26:3

"Peace I leave with you, My peace I give to you; not as the world gives do I give to you. Let not your heart be troubled, neither let it be afraid."

JOHN 14:27

The things which you learned and received and heard and saw in me, these do, and the God of peace will be with you.

PHILIPPIANS 4:9

Now may the Lord of peace Himself give you peace always in every way. The Lord be with you all.

2 THESSALONIANS 3:16

PRAYER

"In this manner, therefore, pray: Our Father in heaven, hallowed be Your name. Your kingdom come. Your will be done on earth as it is in heaven. Give us this day our daily bread. And forgive us our debts, as we forgive our debtors. And do not lead us into temptation, but deliver us from the evil one. For Yours is the kingdom and the power and the glory forever. Amen."

MATTHEW 6:9–13

Praying always with all prayer and supplication in the Spirit, being watchful to this end with all perseverance and supplication for all the saints.

EPHESIANS 6:18

Pray without ceasing.

1 THESSALONIANS 5:17

Let us therefore come boldly to the throne of grace, that we may obtain mercy and find grace to help in time of need.

HEBREWS 4:16

Now this is the confidence that we have in Him, that if we ask anything according to His will, He hears us. And if we know that He hears us, whatever we ask, we know that we have the petitions that we have asked of Him.

1 JOHN 5:14–15

TRUST

And those who know Your name will put their trust in You; for You, LORD, have not forsaken those who seek You.

PSALM 9:10

The LORD is my strength and my shield; my heart trusted in Him, and I am helped; therefore my heart greatly rejoices, and with my song I will praise Him.

PSALM 28:7

He who dwells in the secret place of the Most High shall abide under the shadow of the Almighty. I will say of the Lord, "He is my refuge and my fortress; my God, in Him I will trust."

PSALM 91:1–2

Trust in the Lord with all your heart, and lean not on your own understanding; in all your ways acknowledge Him, and He shall direct your paths.

PROVERBS 3:5–6

The fear of man brings a snare, but whoever trusts in the Lord shall be safe.

PROVERBS 29:25

NOTES

INTRODUCTION

1. Andrew Carroll, "Hear, Hear: David McCullough's Soaring Speeches," *Los Angeles Review of Books*, May 12, 2017, https://lareviewofbooks.org/article/hear-hear-david-mcculloughs-soaring-speeches/.
2. Sinclair Ferguson, *Faithful God: An Exposition of the Book of Ruth* (Darlington, UK: Evangelical Press, 2005), 56–57.
3. R. Kent Hughes, *1001 Great Stories and Quotes* (Wheaton, IL: Tyndale House Publishers, 1998), 255–56.

CHAPTER 1

1. Tom Perrotta and Terry Gross, "After the Rapture, Who Are the 'LNotes
2. *9/11: One Day in America*, episode 1, "First Response," directed by Daniel Bogado, aired on August 29, 2021, accessed on Hulu, https://www.imdb.com/title/tt14734550/.

3. *Merriam-Webster*, s.v., "rapture," accessed February 9, 2022, https://www.merriam-webster.com/dictionary/rapture.

4. Dr. Arnold G. Fruchtenbaum, *The Footsteps of the Messiah: A Study of the Sequence of Prophetic Events* (San Antonio, TX: Ariel Press, 2004), 149.

5. "Religion: Promises," *TIME*, December 24, 1956, http://content.time.com/time/subscriber/article/0,33009,808851,00.html.

6. Max Lucado, *Unshakeable Hope: Building Our Lives on the Promises of God* (Nashville: Thomas Nelson, 2018), 13.

7. Arthur T. Pierson, *The Gospel*, vol. 3 (Grand Rapids, MI: Baker Book House, 1978), 136.

CHAPTER 2

1. Charles H. Dyer, *World News and Bible Prophecy* (Wheaton, IL: Tyndale House Publishers, 1995), 214.

2. A. T. Robertson, *Word Pictures in the New Testament*, s.v. "Matt. 13:21," Christian Classics Ethereal Library, accessed January 7, 2022, http://www.ccel.org/ccel/robertson_at/word.iv.xii.html?highlight=tribulation#highlight.

3. N. T. Wright, quoted in "The Necessity of God's Wrath," *Preaching Today*, accessed January 7, 2022, http://www.preachingtoday.com/illustrations/2009/september/6092809.html.

4. Laura Kusisto and Arian Campo-Flores, "Homes Built to Stricter Standards Fared Better in Storm," *Wall Street Journal*, September 16, 2017, https://www.wsj.com/articles/one-early-lesson-from-irma-hurricane-building-codes-work-1505559600.

CHAPTER 3

1. Steven J. Cole, "Lesson 15: When God's Axe Falls (2 Corinthians 36)," Bible.org, September 9, 2013, https://bible.org/seriespage/lesson-15-when-god-s-axe-falls-2-chronicles-36.

2. Charles R. Swindoll, *Swindoll's Living Insights New Testament Commentary: Revelation* (Carol Stream, IL: Tyndale, 2014), 111.

3. Jim Collins, "The Stockdale Paradox," Jim Collins, accessed January 7, 2022, https://www.jimcollins.com/concepts/Stockdale-Concept.html.

CHAPTER 4

1. Grant R. Jeffrey, *Prince of Darkness: Antichrist and the New World Order* (Toronto: Frontier Research Publications, 1994), 29.

2. John Phillips, *Exploring Revelation* (Neptune, NJ: Loizeaux Brothers, 1991), 166.

3. Charles Colson, *Kingdoms in Conflict* (Grand Rapids, MI: Zondervan, 1987), 131.

4. John Phillips, *Exploring the Future: A Comprehensive Guide to Bible Prophecy* (Grand Rapids: Kregel Publications, 2003), 272.

5. Colson, *Kingdoms in Conflict*, 68.

6. Colson, 68.

7. Thomas Ice, "The Ethnicity of the Antichrist," Pre-Trib Research Center, accessed January 7, 2022, https://www.pre-trib.org/articles/all-articles/message/the-ethnicity-of-the-antichrist/read.

8. Major Dan, "'Goddesses of Reason' Replace Catholic Church in France!," History and Headlines, November 10, 2014, http://www.historyandheadlines.com/goddesses-reason-replace-catholic-church-france/.

9. W. A. Criswell, *Expository Sermons on Revelation,* vol. 4 (Dallas: Criswell Publishing, 1995), 109.

10. Mark Hitchcock, *The End of Money: Bible Prophecy and the Coming Economic Collapse* (Eugene, OR: Harvest House Publishers, 2013), 118–19.

11. *The Omen*, directed by Richard Donner (Los Angeles: Twentieth Century Fox, 1976), https://www.imdb.com/title/tt0075005/.

CHAPTER 5

1. Holocaust Encyclopedia, s.v. "Jakob Frenkiel," accessed January 7, 2022, https://encyclopedia.ushmm.org/content/en/id-card/jakob-frenkiel.

2. George Rosenthal, "Auschwitz-Birkenau: The Evolution of Tattooing in the Auschwitz Concentration Camp Complex," Jewish Virtual Library, accessed January 7, 2022, https://www.jewishvirtuallibrary.org/the-evolution-of-tattooing-in-the-auschwitz-concentration-camp-complex.

3. William F. Arndt and F. W. Gingrich, *A Greek-English Lexicon of the New Testament* (Chicago: University of Chicago Press, 1957), 876.

4. Robert L. Thomas, *Revelation 8–22: An Exegetical Commentary* (Chicago: Moody Press, 1995), 181.

5. Richard Bauckham, *Climax of Prophecy: Studies in the Book of Revelation* (Edinburgh: T. & T. Clark, 1993), 424–25.

6. Tim Chester, *The Ordinary Hero* (Nottingham, England: Intervarsity Press, 2009), 208.

7. Chester, *Ordinary Hero*, 208.

8. J. Scott Duvall, *The Heart of Revelation: Understanding the 10 Essential Themes of the Bible's Final Book* (Grand Rapids, MI: Baker Books, 2016), 190.

CHAPTER 6

1. "The Loss of USS S-4 (SS-109)," Submarine Force Library and Museum Association, December 17, 2013, https://ussnautilus.org /the-loss-of-uss-s-4-ss-109/.

2. Sam Roberts, "Dean Hess, Preacher and Fighter Pilot, Dies at 97," *New York Times*, March 7, 2015, https://www.nytimes .com/2015/03/08/us/dean-hess-preacher-and-fighter-pilot-dies-at-97.html.

3. "Fact Sheet: Col. Dean Hess," National Museum of the US Air Force, accessed September 25, 2018, https://web.archive.org /web/20100416203427/http://www.nationalmuseum.af.mil /factsheets/factsheet.asp?id=1913.

4. Henry M. Morris, *The Revelation Record* (Wheaton, IL: Tyndale House Publishers, 1983), 119.

5. Leonard Griffith, *God in Man's Experience* (Waco, TX; Word Books, 1968), 175.

6. Tim Chester, *The Ordinary Hero* (Nottingham, England: Intervarsity Press, 2009), 207.

7. Paul W. Powell, *The Night Cometh* (Tyler, TX: Paul W. Powell, 2002), 10, 18.

CHAPTER 7

1. Tim LaHaye and Jerry Jenkins, *Are We Living in the End Times? Current Events Foretold in Scripture...And What They Mean* (Wheaton, IL: Tyndale House Publishers, 2011), 222.

2. Based on Sir Ernest Henry Shackleton, *South: The Story of Shackleton's Last Expedition, 1914–1917* (New York: MacMillan Co., 1920), Project Gutenberg, accessed January 7, 2022, http:// www.gutenberg.org/ebooks/5199.

3. Harry A. Ironside, *Revelation* (Grand Rapids, MI: Kregel, 2004), 187–88.

4. Robert J. Morgan, *My All in All* (Nashville: B&H, 2008), entry for July 16.

5. Ironside, *Revelation*, 189–90.

6. John F. Walvoord, *End Times: Understanding Today's World Events in Biblical Prophecy* (Nashville: Word Publishing, 1998), 171.

CHAPTER 8

1. Marguerite Higgins, *War in Korea: The Report of a Woman Combat Correspondent* (New York: Doubleday, 1951).

2. Randy Alcorn, *Heaven* (Wheaton, IL: Tyndale, 2004), 226.

3. Alcorn, *Heaven*, 101.

4. Quoted in Richard Leonard and JoNancy Linn Sundberg, *A Glimpse of Heaven* (New York: Howard, 2007), 45.

5. Charles F. Pfeiffer and Everett F. Harrison, eds., *The Wycliffe Bible Commentary: A Phrase by Phrase Commentary of the Bible* (Chicago: Moody Publishers, 1962), 1522.

6. "Land of the Dying," Bible.org, February 2, 2009, https://bible.org/illustration/land-dying.

7. There are several versions of this story, but the main storyline in all the variations is the same; "The Little Boy Who Put the World Back Together: A Story by Jim Quinn, Founder of Lifestream Basic Seminar," Cameron Freeman, accessed January 7, 2022, https://cameronfreeman.com/personal/confessions-cult-leader-lifestream-seminar-experience/boy-put-world-story-jim-quinn-founder-lifestream-basic-seminar/.

ABOUT THE AUTHOR

DR. DAVID JEREMIAH IS THE FOUNDER OF TURNING POINT, AN INTER-national ministry committed to providing Christians with sound Bible teaching through radio and television, the internet, live events, and resource materials and books. He is the author of more than fifty books, including *Overcomer, A Life Beyond Amazing, Is This the End?, The Spiritual Warfare Answer Book, David Jeremiah Morning and Evening Devotions, Airship Genesis Kids Study Bible,* and *The Jeremiah Study Bible.*

Dr. Jeremiah serves as the senior pastor of Shadow Mountain Community Church in El Cajon, California, where he resides with his wife, Donna. They have four grown children and twelve grandchildren. Connect with Dr. Jeremiah on Facebook (@drdavidjeremiah), Twitter (@davidjeremiah), and on his website (davidjeremiah.org).

stay connected to the teaching of

DR. DAVID JEREMIAH

• • • • • • • •

Publishing | Radio | Television | Online

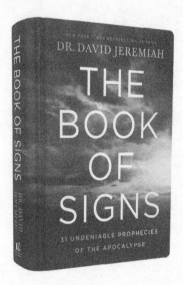

Also Available from Dr. David Jeremiah

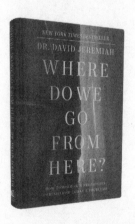